BORDER COLLIE

SMART OWNER'S GUIDE®

By Wendy Bedwell-Wilson

FROM THE EDITORS OF DOGFANCY® MAGAZINE

CONTENTS

Border Collie, a Smart Owner's Guide®

ISBN: 978-1-593787-82-0 (Hardcover) ©2012
ISBN: 978-1-593787-94-3 (Softcover) ©2012

All rights reserved. No part of this book may be reproduced in any form, by Photostat, scanner, microfilm, xerography, or any other means, or incorporated into any information retrieval system, electronic or mechanical, without the written permission of the copyright owner.

photographers include Isabelle Francais; Tara Darling; Gina Cioli; Shutterstock.com

For CIP information, see page 176.
Printed in China.

I f you are considering bringing a Border Collie into your life, congratulations! You're in good company. This breed's incredible intelligence, energy, trainability, and work ethic are what have catapulted it to worldwide popularity in recent years. From print ads and movies to TV series and all manner of commercials, the Border Collie has become the poster pup for brainy dogs in the media. Where chic Afghan Hounds and Poodles once dominated the fashion and lifestyle pages, today it's the Border Collie who's lounging on leather sofas, dining in state-of-the-art kitchens, and riding in luxury SUVs.

Fantasy has its place, but for prospective dog owners, a reality check is in order—never more so than when investigating the Border Collie. The same qualities that make this breed such an asset on the farm and agility course present a huge challenge to pet owners. A Border Collie can make a wonderful companion in the right home, but the breed's prey drive and relentless energy are difficult to live with. This is a dog who must have an active, engaged owner who accepts the commitment to keep him busy, well exercised, and always with a job to do. The Border Collie may be considered the world's most intelligent dog, but he doesn't train himself.

Much like a gifted child who isn't challenged in school, a bored, neglected Border Collie will become destructive. Confinement and isolation lead to barking, digging, and chewing. Small, furry pets and running children will trigger the dog's prey-chasing instinct, often with tragic consequences.

Remember that the breed's temperament was irrelevant to the shepherds who lived alone on the hills and moors. A shy or wary dog was a non-issue in an isolated environment. That's not the case for modern-day owners in suburbia. Early and ongoing socialization of puppies is essential to prevent shyness or aggression.

A Border Collie is in his element when he's doing what he was meant to do.

Where you acquire your puppy is always of prime importance, but particularly so in this breed because different bloodlines display different behaviors. Those bloodlines bred to work cattle tend to produce stubborn, dominant dogs. Many bloodlines that work sheep and compete in trials produce softer, more responsive dogs. The most successful obedience dogs are intense and high-energy and love to retrieve. Border Collies descended from conformation (dog show) bloodlines are generally more mellow, with less prey drive, and probably make the best pets.

The parents of a litter will give you an excellent indication of how the puppies will turn out. You won't have the parents to meet and observe if you adopt your dog from a shelter or Border Collie rescue group, so in this case, try to obtain as much information as you can about the dog's past. How did the rescue volunteers acquire him? What do they know about his background? What light can the foster home shed on his individual quirks? How is he with children, adults, men, women, other pets, riding in the car, being left alone? The more observations they can share with you, the better equipped you will be to choose the right Border Collie.

The Border Collie is indeed unique, but that means that he isn't right for everyone. Take the time to study the breed and assess your family to ensure that you and the Border Collie really are the best fit. There are lots of great breeds out there to consider, many of them much less complex and demanding in their care. If you are convinced that the Border Collie is the one for

JOIN OUR ONLINE Club Border™

With this Smart Owner's Guide®, you are well on your way to earning your Border Collie diploma. But your Border Collie education doesn't end here. You are invited to join **Club Border™** (**DogChannel.com/Club-Border**), a FREE online site with lots of fun and instructive features, such as:

◆ **forums, blogs,** and **profiles** where you can connect with other Border Collie owners
◆ **downloadable charts** and **checklists** to help you be a smart and loving dog owner
◆ access to Border Collie **e-cards** and **wallpapers**
◆ interactive **games**
◆ canine **quizzes**

The **Smart Owner's Guide** series and **Club Border** are backed by the experts at DOG FANCY® magazine and DogChannel.com—who have been providing trusted and up-to-date information about dogs and dog people for more than forty years. Log on and join the club today!

you, proceed with caution, talk to breeders and owners, and find the most suitable dog for your family's energy level.

Allan Reznik
Editor-at-Large, DOG FANCY

CHAPTER 1

THE BRAINY

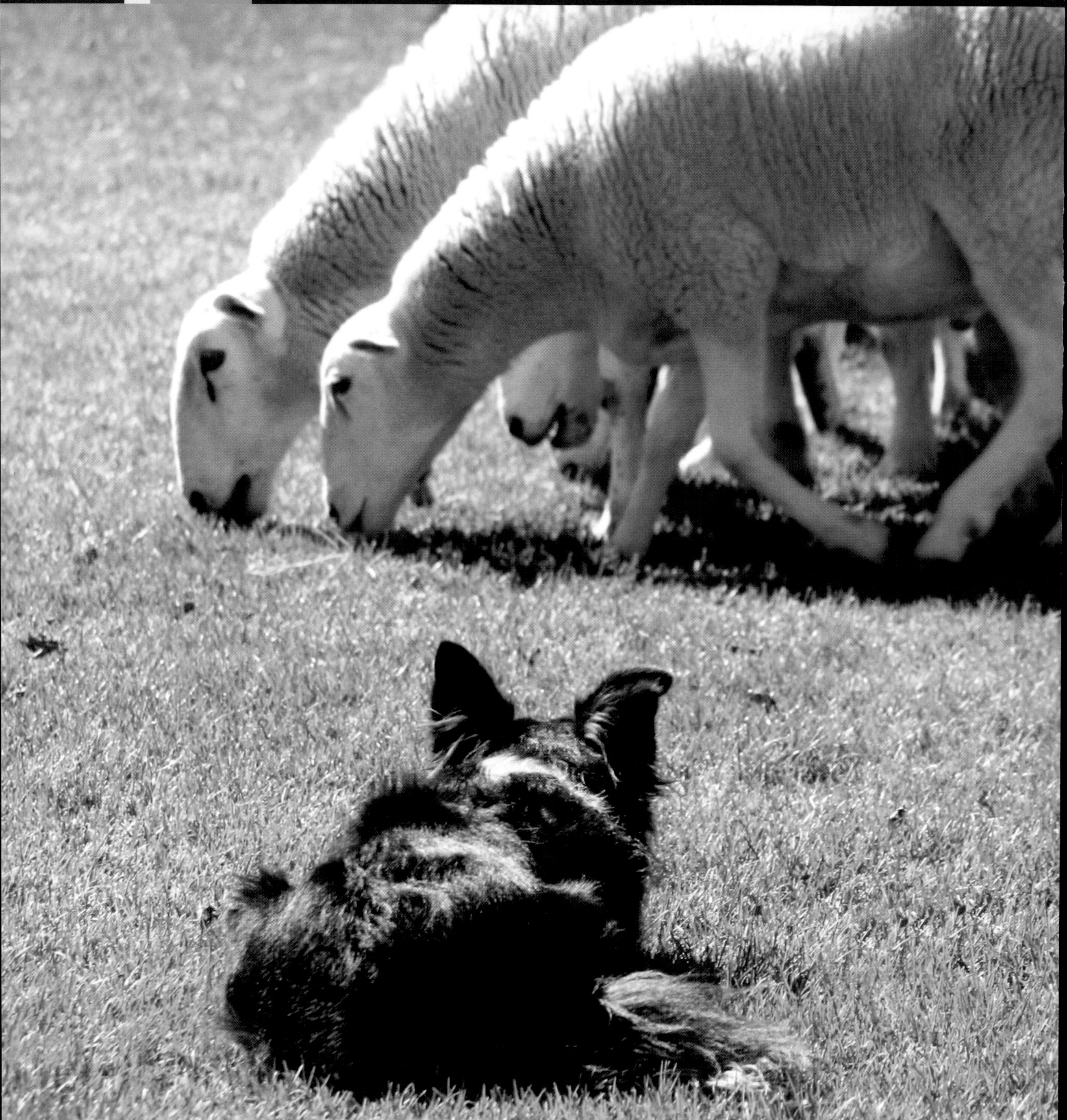

It's six o'clock in the morning; the sun is just peeking over the horizon. "It's time for work, Sparky," calls out the sheep rancher. His three-year-old tricolor Border Collie jumps from her bed and dashes to the door, her long tail wagging in anticipation. This dog knows the meaning of *work*—and it's her favorite thing to do. Sparky lives for heading off herds, circling behind them, and driving them from field to field with her hypnotic eyes.

Border Collies are working dogs, and through the centuries of their companionship with humans, they have been selectively bred for intelligence and versatility. They're trusted dogs who work alongside shepherds, keeping watch over livestock and moving sheep and cattle from field to field. Border Collies are he best employees a rancher could ask for.

Border Collies make wonderful working companions and stock keepers' helpers; they are not considered simply house pets. This tireless, high-energy breed requires owners who are committed to giving their dog a stimulating and challenging job.

Did You Know? **Border Collies differ from other herding breeds, such as the Australian Cattle Dog and German Shepherd Dog**, in that they drive the flock toward the handler from behind rather than nipping at the animals' heels and barking, driving animals away from the handler.

Whether your Border Collie spends his days herding a flock of ewes, practicing and competing in agility, or going on several energy-expending walks a day with you, he needs an active pursuit. If Border Collies don't find meaningful work, they'll become bored and depressed.

Border Collies are highly intelligent, hardworking, tenacious, active, trainable—the list goes on. Unlike some breeds, which were developed for a specific body conformation and look, the Border Collie has been selectively bred for intelligence and trainability. Let's take a closer look at what makes this workaholic, high-IQ dog tick; what sets the breed apart from its canine cousins; and what characteristics the ideal Border Collie family should have.

SMARTS AND LOYALTY

Examples of the breed's wit and ingenuity are legendary. Take Rico, for example. This Border Collie made news in the 1990s when animal psychologist Juliane Kaminski from the Max Planck Institute for Evolutionary Anthropology in Leipzig, Germany, investigated the claim that Rico could understand more than two hundred simple words that referred to specific items. To test the dog's skills, Kaminski first randomly divided the items into twenty sets of ten items. Next, she arranged one ten-item set in an experiment room. She then joined Rico and his owner in an adjoining room and asked the owner to command Rico to bring back two specific items from the experiment room. Kaminski repeated the exercise with the remaining sets of items and documented the results, which showed that Rico retrieved an average of thirty-seven out of forty items correctly.

Betsy, another Border Collie, usurped Rico's reign with her 340-word vocabulary. At just ten weeks old, the puppy could reportedly sit on command and retrieve a variety of objects by name. She could detect speech inflections, make a connection between a photograph and the physical object it represented, and recognize people by name.

Widely considered to be one of the most intelligent dog breeds, the Border Collie has a brain that seems to never stop churning. In fact, psychologist Stanley Coren reports in his book *The Intelligence of Dogs* that the Border Collie is the most intelligent breed of dog. In the field, Border Collies are thinking about managing the flock. On the farm, they're keeping an eye on the chickens and goats. And in the home, they're concocting ways to entertain themselves—which may mean that they're rearranging your living room.

Owners of these brilliant Border Collies can train their dogs to do virtually anything. In addition to being top-rated herding dogs and tenders of livestock, Border Collies excel at dog sports, such as agility, obedience, and rally. They hunt alongside gundogs. They make compassionate therapy and assistance dogs. They contribute their tracking and scenting prowess to search and rescue efforts. This breed can do it all.

While the Border Collie's intelligence makes him well suited to any task, those smarts can prove a challenge for some owners to handle. To harness and shape your Border Collie's brain, you'll need to train him—and then some. He'll need to learn basic manners and obedience before you progress to any specialty training for activities such as herding or flyball. Whatever you do with your Border Collie, you'll need to learn how to keep his sharp mind engaged and stimulated.

Bred to be working companions, Border Collies are devoted to their owners. They're eager to please, and they live for excelling in their profession. As such, the breed has developed a discerning eye for taking cues from humans. Because early ancestors of the Border Collie had to be able to respond to whistles or hand signals from hundreds of yards away, the dogs eventually learned how to read their owners' moods and expressions.

That seemingly innate connection with their owners means that Border Collies also make committed companions both in the field and in the home. They live to work, to play, and to rest alongside their owners, wanting to spend quality time with their humans doing whatever it is that they're doing. In many cases, a Border Collie will be a human's shadow, taking direction from his owner and always looking for ways to "help."

KEEP HIM MOVING

They're brilliant, yes, but keep in mind that Border Collies also need outlets for their boundless energy. Always on the move, these dogs bore from inactivity, which can get them into trouble. Many think of Border Collies as hyperactive, but it's likely that all they need is a long day in the field or a few hours of fast-paced agility practice to calm down. The owner must know how to prevent boredom.

One Border Collie owner complained that her dog, a one-year-old female, wouldn't stop wiggling and pacing indoors. The dog would also incessantly gnaw on her bed and pull the stuffing out of all of her toys. The owner worried that something was wrong with the dog, but the problem was that the woman worked a full-time job and left her pup alone all day. When the woman returned from work, she would let her dog out into the yard for a little while and then spend the rest of the evening with her dog, cooking dinner and reading. It's no wonder the dog was constantly moving around and even engaging in destructive behaviors—she suffered from pent-up energy. Once the owner realized that her lifestyle didn't suit the emotional and physical needs of the dog, she was lucky to find a good home for the dog on a farm with a family who had livestock.

This is not to say that Border Collies can't thrive in the suburbs; they will be content as long as they get regular, vigorous exercise. An active household filled with high-energy humans and plenty of room to run makes an ideal home for the breed. Border Collie owners don't need to be farmers or ranchers, but they should be engaged in lots of outdoor activities, including hiking, playing Frisbee, going on long walks through the neighborhood, and competing in dog sports such as agility and flyball. To replicate the herding lifestyle that he's been bred to lead, a nonworking

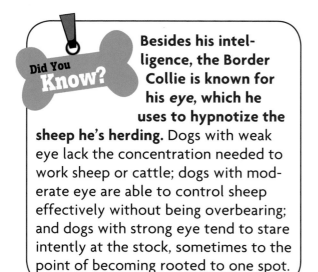

Did You Know?

Besides his intelligence, the Border Collie is known for his *eye*, which he uses to hypnotize the sheep he's herding. Dogs with weak eye lack the concentration needed to work sheep or cattle; dogs with moderate eye are able to control sheep effectively without being overbearing; and dogs with strong eye tend to stare intently at the stock, sometimes to the point of becoming rooted to one spot.

The drive to work makes these dogs unique. It is a force of nature [that] we alter to fit our needs. Training a stock dog is much like changing the course of a stream or river; we can change its path to fit our needs but cannot stop the flow.

—Bruce Fogt, a Border Collie owner and trainer in Sidney, Ohio

Enlist the help of responsible family and friends when planning activities for your Border Collie. Ask your son to toss the Frisbee with your pup for an hour. Invite your niece to take him to the beach for some afternoon fun. Ask your spouse to take him to the store for some out-and-about time. Your dog will love the attention and the action!

Border Collie requires hours of stimulation to occupy his brain and body, similar to what he would get from herding a flock of sheep all day long.

Because this breed has such high activity demands, it's critical for potential owners to know what they're getting into before acquiring a Border Collie. They should do their research about a Border Collie's activity requirements, examine their own lifestyles and habits, and determine whether the breed is a good match for them long before starting to look for breeders or dogs for adoption. If someone acquires a Border Collie and realizes that the dog is too much to handle, rehoming the dog can be an emotional trial for the owner and the dog. Rehoming or surrendering a dog is a potentially painful experience that is unfair to the dog and that can be prevented through early, honest evaluation of the owner's expectations and the dog's needs.

A "STANDARD" LOOK

Besides having a personality and temperament all its own, the Border Collie also has a distinct look that differentiates the breed from other dogs. This look is based on the breed standard, which is the written description of the hypothetically "perfect" Border Collie. The standard defines the trademark characteristics of the breed, sets forth desirable and undesirable traits, and explains the breed's background and what makes the breed what it is.

Breed clubs develop these written standards, which are then submitted to the purebred dog registries. Different countries have different registries; in the United States, the largest purebred registries are the American Kennel Club (AKC) and the United Kennel Club (UKC). Judges use these breed standards to evaluate dogs at competitive events sponsored by the respective registries.

The traits discussed as follows are based on the requirements of the AKC standard, which became effective on March 2, 2004, and was written by the Border Collie Society of America, the AKC parent club for the Border Collie.

In general, Border Collies are medium-sized, alert dogs who are athletic, graceful, and agile. Their muscular bodies have a smooth outline that conveys the impression of effortless movement and endless endurance. Above all else, however, the Border Collie's conformation, or physical features, should enhance the breed's ability to be a true working herding dog. Nothing should impede the dog's ability to do the job for which he was intended.

Body and bone structure: Measuring 19 to 22 inches at the withers (or shoulder blades) for males and 18 to 21 inches for females, Border Collies have strong yet light bones that create a balanced and proportionate silhouette. A Border Collie should be large enough to be taken seriously by other animals but small enough to move easily and quickly as needed. The

An active Border Collie is a content Border Collie! This energetic breed thrives on having a job to do.

body, including the neck, topline, forequarters, and hindquarters, should be strong and sturdy enough to handle the rigorous demands of herding for hours at a time.

Expression: The expression, eyes, and ears all suggest a dog who is full of energy and intensity. Border Collies exude intelligence, alertness, eagerness, and interest. The oval, moderately sized eyes can be any shade of brown and occasionally are seen in blue. The medium-sized ears may be erect or dropped, and they are mobile, picking up the slightest sound. The Border Collie's moderately wide skull con-

tains that legendary brain, and the strong muzzle tapers slightly to the nose, the color of which matches the dog's primary body color.

Tail: Border Collies carry their tails low when working. A tail carried high over their back, which is known as a "gay" or "cocky" tail, can distract the sheep, making it impossible for the dog to stare down and control the flock with his hypnotic eyes. Some trainers feel that a tail carried high indicates a lack of concentration. However, a Border Collie will sometimes carry his tail proudly in a display of confidence.

Coat and color: Two coat types—rough and smooth—are seen in the Border Collie. Both types of coat feature close-fitting, dense, weather-resistant double coats in which the top coat is either straight or wavy. The rough variety is medium length with feathering on the forelegs, haunches, chest, and underside and short hair on the face, ears, feet, and fronts of legs. The smooth coat is short all over and may have a little feathering on the forelegs, haunches, chest, and ruff.

As far as coat color and pattern, just about anything goes. Border Collie coats may appear in all sorts of colors and combinations, including solid colors, bicolors, tricolors, merle (a marbled pattern), and sable (black-tipped hairs on parts of the body).

Border Collies often have white patches, commonly on the legs, on the chest, and/or as a blaze on the face, which may or may not have ticking. In terms of conformation, color and markings always take a backseat to physical structure and movement.

WORKING MOVES

Speaking of movement, the Border Collie breed standard also describes the dog's gait, or the way the dog moves. When working, a Border Collie typically uses two gaits: a gallop and a moving crouch. In the crouching motion, the dogs carry their heads level or slightly below their shoulder blades, creating that unique Border Collie look. At a trot, the Border Collie's stride should be balanced and fluid so that he glides effortlessly over the ground. As the dog increases his speed while trotting, his feet converge under the center line of gravity until they follow a single track.

Gait in a working dog such as the Border Collie is of utmost importance, as it is the supreme test of bone structure and function. A choppy or prancing gait, although fun to watch, is impractical and causes the working dog to tire rapidly.

IS IT A MATCH?

As you can see, Border Collies are built to live in an environment where they can do what they do best: herd livestock. To thrive physically, mentally, and emotionally, these dogs need jobs, they need space in which to do their jobs, and they need owners who understand the breed's need for hours of challenging activities each day.

Are you ready to welcome this high-energy dog into your life? Do you have what it takes to keep up with a Border Collie? Before you bring a puppy or adult Border Collie home, take a very close look

Did You Know?

The Border Collie doesn't just have a keen eye; the breed also has very sensitive hearing. Early shepherds and breeders naturally selected dogs with acute hearing so that the animals could keep an eye on their flocks while simultaneously obeying verbal commands. In the field, this trait is a valuable one when the dog needs to distinguish handler commands from background noise; in the home, though, it could translate into the dog's being overly sensitive or uncomfortable around loud noises, such as thunder or fireworks. Some Border Collies will even move themselves to a quiet place when something on television is too loud or intense.

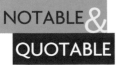
Apart from his work, there is not much to be said about the Border Collie.

—A. Croxton Smith, a leading British canine authority, quoted
in Tim Longton and Edward Hart's book The Sheep Dog, Its Work and Training

at your expectations and lifestyle. Your family's activity level and pastimes should match those of your chosen breed—and if they're not aligned, you'd do best to consider another breed.

When making your decision, think about the following:

- What are you planning to do with your dog? If you're looking for a ranch hand or a companion to herd your sheep or livestock, this could be the dog for you. You still can be a suitable Border Collie owner even if you don't have flocks to herd, but you must be prepared to be very active with your pet, engaging your Border Collie's body and mind. If you're looking for a furry friend who will watch football games on TV with you, another breed may be in order.
- Do you have room for your dog to roam safely? Do you live on a farm or ranch or have a large backyard? Is your property fenced? If so, then you have space for a Border Collie to stretch his legs. Even if you don't have land, you can still give your dog the exercise he needs by

taking him on challenging trail hikes, for runs on the beach, or for romps on the agility course. He just needs access to places where he can burn off some energy.

- Is someone at home during the day? Because this breed lives to work, a Border Collie needs mental and physical stimulation provided by a job or an attentive human. A lonely, bored Border Collie can be trouble. If you or your family's schedule means that no one will be home for extended periods during the day, you should bring your Border Collie to a doggy day care facility or arrange for a dog walker to come by regularly to give your dog exercise, companionship, and bathroom breaks.
- Do you have the time to dedicate to training? In order for a Border Collie (or any dog, for that matter) to integrate into your household, you'll need to teach him some basic manners and obedience skills—and practice them regularly. Most Border Collie owners keep up with training throughout their dogs' lives with agility, obedience, or other types of advanced training.
- Do you (or your family members) have time to keep up with the daily chores related to your Border Collie's care? Who will be responsible for feeding and watering the dog? Who will take him outside to go to the bathroom? Who will brush him, take him for daily walks, and be in charge of his training sessions?

Of course, every family and every situation is different, but in general, a prospective Border Collie owner should be prepared to dedicate a good amount of time to training and being very active with his or her dog.

The Border Collie is always up for a game with his favorite person!

Show your artistic side. Share photos, videos, and artwork of your favorite breed at Club Border. You can also submit jokes, riddles, and even poetry about Border Collies. Browse through our galleries and see the talent of fellow Border owners. Go to **DogChannel.com/ Club-Border** and click on "Galleries" to get started.

One Eager Partner

Paige, a four-year-old Border Collie in Fairfax, Virginia, loves to lend a hand—well, a paw—around the house. Her owner, Lauren Girard, works as a chemist at the Food and Drug Administration's Center for Veterinary Medicine, so Paige plays house mom.

Luckily, Paige is a good girl while Girard is away from home.

"Paige stays at home when I'm at work during the day," Girard says. "She's comfortable being alone when I'm gone. When I get home, I usually take her out, and we will either work on training, go to a class together, or have a long play session outside."

Girard's hobby and passion is training her high-IQ pup. Some of the tricks she's taught Paige include gathering laundry and carrying it to the washing machine in her mouth; putting away groceries by pulling open the refrigerator door using a dish towel hanging from the handle and depositing the food inside; and tucking herself in at night by jumping onto her bed, lying down, grabbing one corner of her blanket, and wrapping herself up like a burrito. Paige even helps Girard with the dishes, passing the dirty plates to Girard while she's washing them.

When Girard brought Paige home as a puppy, she enrolled Paige in obedience class, where she took top honors. Before long, Paige had learned how to lie down and roll over, and within weeks, she had mastered tasks such as picking up her toys and putting them in her toy box.

"Paige is off-the-charts smart and energetic," Girard says. "It brings me so much joy to have such a bright and eager partner."

Your Border Collie will happily join you in your outdoor activities.

BORDER COLLIE BASICS

This herding dog has it all!

COUNTRY OF ORIGIN: Great Britain

WHAT HIS FRIENDS CALL HIM: BC, Collie, Workaholic

SIZE: Males: 19 to 22 inches, 45 pounds; females: 18 to 21 inches, 40 pounds (height measured at shoulder)

OVERALL APPEARANCE: Medium in size and athletic with a smooth, muscular outline

COAT: Dense double coat with a coarse top coat; seen in rough and smooth varieties

COLOR: Solid colors, bicolors, tricolors, merles, and sables are seen in the breed, all with or without white markings, which may have ticking

PERSONALITY TRAITS: Intelligent, hardworking, athletic, loyal, tenacious, sensitive

WITH KIDS: Best with older children under supervision and with training; may try to herd younger children

WITH OTHER ANIMALS: Generally good with supervision

ENERGY LEVEL: Very high; requires several hours of vigorous daily activity to keep boredom and resultant mischief in check

GROOMING NEEDS: Daily brushing of the coat and teeth; bathing and nail clipping as needed; regular checks of the eyes and ears

TRAINABILITY: Very high; the breed responds well to positive training techniques

LIVING ENVIRONMENT: Does best on a farm or ranch or in a suburban home with a fenced backyard and ample opportunity to exercise

LIFESPAN: Average 12 to 15 years

The Border Collie enjoys a rich, long heritage that stretches back to times when people first began raising and keeping domesticated livestock. Farmers' and ranchers' constant companions, these herding dogs worked sheep and cattle, guarded the flocks, and kept their human caretakers company.

Though the actual origin of the breed will probably never be known for certain, we do know that early Border Collie-like dogs existed in Europe thousands of years ago, eventually developing into the workaholics we know today.

In this chapter, let's explore the origins of Border Collies, how these dogs have changed over time, and why they've captured our interest today.

A LONG LOOK BACK

Dogs have served alongside humans for thousands of years as protectors, helpers, and best friends. From their wild wolf beginnings, they learned to live with humans, and as they became domesticated, people discovered that they were indispensable companions.

The American Kennel Club recognized the Border Collie as a distinct breed in 1995, categorizing it in its Herding Group. Before that, the registry listed the breed in its Miscellaneous Class for more than fifty years.

it's a Fact

As far back as 36 BC, humans used dogs to help them on their farms. Roman historians Cato and Varro detailed herding dogs, their role on the farm, and their proper care in their book *De Re Rustica*, in which they described large, heavy-boned dogs who herded and protected flocks and who had black, tan, and, white rough (long) or smooth (short) coats. These Roman herding dogs attacked and fought silently so as not to alarm their charges. This type of dog preceded not only the Border Collie but also several other breeds, including the Rottweiler, Bernese Mountain Dog, and Great Pyrenees.

When the Roman armies invaded Britain in 55 BC and marched across the British countryside, they brought along their herding dogs to fend off wolves and other predators and to protect and steer the livestock used to feed the men. Early handlers also used them as multipurpose helpers and drovers' dogs (dogs that drive livestock from one place to another). Some of these Border Collie forebears ran away from their owners or were freed after their services were no longer needed, and they found homes throughout the British Isles, thriving across the countryside.

When the Roman Empire began to crumble 700 years later, the Vikings from Scandinavia increasingly raided Britain. In AD 794, when the marauders successfully invaded Scotland and Ireland and began settling, they brought with them spitz-type dogs that they used for herding. These dogs weighed 25 to 35 pounds and were usually black or sable in color with white markings. They had short, dense double coats; prick ears; fox-like faces; and, often, blue eyes.

Over a period of years, farmers crossed these small spitz-type dogs with descendents of the Romans' larger herding dogs. They discovered that the smaller size and lighter bone structure of the hybrid proved advantageous in the Scottish Highlands and Wales, where the rocky and hilly terrain preferred by wild mountain sheep demanded an agile and quick dog. These hybrids typically weighed 25 to 35 pounds. In the flat lowlands of Scotland and northern England, however, a taller, heavier dog evolved; these 50- to 65-pound dogs could handle domesticated livestock.

Today, the average Border Collie male weighs about 45 pounds and stands 21 inches tall at the shoulder, with females slightly shorter and lighter. Small dogs of the highland "fox" type and larger dogs of the lowland "farm collie" type still occur today in Scotland and northern England, where the breed originated.

DOCUMENTING THE BREED

A Welsh king called Hywel Dda (or Hywel the Good) provides fanciers with one of the earliest descriptions of the Border Collie. In AD 943, Hywel wrote about a black sheepdog who took a flock of sheep out to graze in the hills and brought them home in the evening. Very impressed by the dog's working skills, the king decreed

Did You Know?

What's in a name? Quite a bit of history, that's what. In the ancient Celtic language, *collie* is similar to one word that means "black" and another that means "faithful." In another dialect, the word equivalent to *collie* means "useful." Most Border Collies are all of the above.

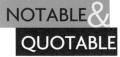
There is something quite magical about watching a shepherd quietly communicate with a Border Collie. With simple, quiet instructions, whistles, or hand gestures, shepherds command their dogs from quite a distance to perform jobs that Border Collies have been performing for hundreds of years.

—Mary Burch, Ph.D., Border Collie fancier, author, and director of the AKC's Canine Good Citizen Program

that a good sheepdog was worth as much as a prime ox—and in those days, that was a fine sum, indeed!

Writings from the 1400s and 1500s further describe dogs resembling the Border Collie. In the *Book of St. Albans*, a collection of essays on hawking, hunting, and heraldry published in 1486, writers called the dogs tryndel tayles, meaning "long-tailed," as opposed to the bob-tailed drover's dogs commonly used in England at the time.

In Dr. Johannes Caius's book *De Canibus Britannicis* (which translates to "Of English Dogges") from 1570, the author provides details about shepherd dogs that would aptly describe modern Border Collies: "This dogge either at the hearing of his masters voyce, or at the wagging and whisteling in his fist, or at his shrill and horse hissing bringeth the wandring weathers and straying sheepe, into the selfe same place where his masters will and wishe is to have the[m], wherby the shepherd repeth

this benefite, namely, that with litle labour and no toyle or moving of his feete he may rule and guide his flocke, according to his owne desire, backward, or to turne this way, or to take that way."

As time passed, more and more authors and artists included Border Collies in their works. In 1790, Thomas Bewick mentioned the Border Collie in his book *The General History of Quadrupeds*, describing the breed as a "rough-coated Collie, black with white tail tip…This breed of dog appears at present to be preserved in the greatest purity in the Northern parts of England and Scotland, where its aid is highly necessary in managing the numerous flocks of sheep in these extensive wilds and fells." In the book, Bewick included woodcut prints depicting dogs that mirror today's Border Collie.

Sydenham Edwards included a watercolor rendering of Border Collies in his book *Cynographia Britannica* from 1800. In the painting, titled *The Shepherd's Dog and the Cur*, three Border Collie-like dogs with black and white flowing coats are pictured alongside a "cur," which he describes as a cross between the "shepherd's dog" and the terrier.

Over the years, the popularity of the Border Collie as a shepherd's helper increased in measure with the rapidly expanding wool industry. As more and more shepherds maintained larger flocks and had greater numbers of livestock, it became impossible for lone shepherds to manage their animals without help. By the early 1800s, Border Collies were becoming regular fixtures on farms and hillsides.

THE FARM AND BEYOND

By the mid-1800s, people were starting to take pride in dog ownership. They wanted to show that they had quality animals, and they were proud to demonstrate their dogs' skills. Organized dog shows began in 1859 in Britain, and by 1865, Collies were appearing in British shows. The Collie at that time came in all shapes and sizes, and there was tremendous variety within the breed.

In the United Kingdom in 1860, the first classes for "Scotch Sheep Dogs" were held at the Birmingham Dog Show Society's National Dog Show, the second dog show held in England. A short time later, Queen Victoria met her first Collie and became an instant fancier. At this point in the breed's history, experts note that the traditional shepherd dog (ancestors of today's Border Collies) and the modern Collie diverged into separate gene pools as individuals began breeding dogs for conformation rather than working ability.

In the 1880s, the historic Collie Club of England formed and developed an evaluation system for all types of Collies, including Border Collies, who had yet to claim that moniker. The Collie Club created a description of how Collies should look as well as a point system that judges were to use when evaluating the dogs' conformation.

As the early breed's popularity continued to grow in the show ring, so did recognition of the dogs' herding skills through sheepdog trials, which are competitive events designed to demonstrate and test livestock-herding ability. The first sheepdog trial of record was held in Bala, Wales,

on October 9, 1873. A Scottish-bred dog named Tweed won the challenge despite the fact that his sheep at one point bolted over a stone wall into the crowds.

Mr. R. J. Lloyd Price has been credited with instituting sheepdog trials. The American Kennel Club notes that "in 1876, Price brought 100 wild Welsh sheep to the Alexandra Palace in London for a demonstration. Three sheep were picked out of the flock, which had been guided to a remote corner of the park, and were carried to a far hill and released. The sheepdogs' responsibilities were to fold the sheep into a small pen in the middle of the park. An account in the *Live Stock Journal* described the astonishment of the spectators at the intelligence of the dogs, whose only assistance was in the form of hand signals and whistles from their masters. It is this astonishing ability which serious Border Collie breeders wish to retain in the breed, above all else."

In July 1906, at a meeting in Haddington, East Lothian, Scotland, the International Sheepdog Society (ISDS) was formed. The society's goals were to stimulate interest in the shepherd and his or her calling, to secure better management of stock by improving the shepherd's dog and his abilities, to hold sheepdog trials, and to

Did You Know?

Several breeds claim the Border Collie in their heritage, including the Shetland Sheepdog, the Smooth Collie, the Rough Collie, the English Shepherd, the Bearded Collie, and the Australian Shepherd. It's no surprise that they're all excellent herding dogs.

develop a studbook to serve as a written record of the dogs' breeding information and lineage.

Until this point, Border Collies answered to an assortment of names, including Shepherd's Dog, Colley Dog, Coally Dog, and plain ol' Collie. These informal names eventually were modified to distinguish dogs from different regions or who performed different jobs, such as Irish, Welsh, or English Collie or Shepherd; Scotch Border Collie; Working Collie; Old-Fashioned Collie; and Farm-Type Collie.

Border Collie became the breed's official name when, in 1915, the secretary of the ISDS, James A. Reid, added the word "Border" to the registration forms. He chose this word because the best working Collies came from the border counties between northern England and southern Scotland. Despite Reid's attempts to accurately identify dogs who were Border Collies, the occasional farmer or shepherd continued to use the old labeling system, listing the dogs simply as "Collies" rather than as "Border Collies."

The late 1800s and early 1900s saw the migration of Border Collies to North America, often accompanying shepherds and livestock moving abroad. Scottish shepherds, such as Sam Stoddard in Oregon

and Idaho and William Millar in the East, helped spread the use of Border Collies in the United States for both sheep and cattle herding. In 1923, Stoddard, who was the resident shepherd for the University of Idaho, acquired Spot, winner of the ISDS's International Supreme Championships. Stoddard, along with other shepherds, helped introduce American stock-raisers and the public to trained Border Collies; most had never seen such skilled dogs.

Stoddard heavily influenced Arthur Allen, who started the North American Sheepdog Society (NASDS) in 1940 and made Spot posthumously the first entry in its stud book. From that point on, working Border Collies grew to become the mainstay of farmers and ranchers in North America.

In the United States, the largest registry is the American Border Collie Association (ABCA), which is dedicated to preserving the working dog's traits rather than focusing on the breed's conformation. Historically, there have been two other work-centric registries: the NASDS and the American International Border Collie registry (AIBC).

The American Kennel Club, the country's largest purebred dog registry, recognized the Border Collie in its Herding Group on October 1, 1995, after more than fifty years of categorizing the breed in its Miscellaneous Class. The AKC parent club for the breed is the Border Collie Society of America (BCSA).

Today, tension still exists between those Border Collie registries that breed solely toward a working standard and those that also emphasize conformation, or physical appearance. The registries focusing on working ability, such as the ABCA, the NASDS, and the AIBC, allow cross-registration among themselves; however, the aforementioned groups do not recognize

those dogs with AKC pedigrees. The AKC does accept dogs who are registered with the ABCA, AIBC, and NASDS.

BORDER COLLIES TODAY

Since the early days of sheepdog trials, the drive, intelligence, and trainability of the Border Collie have been noted by far more people than just shepherds. Today, the Border Collie is one of the most popular and successful breeds in obedience and agility competitions. In fact, in *The Intelligence of Dogs*, Stanley Coren lists the Border Collie as the brightest dog breed. After surveying dog trainers, he found that Border Collies ranked highest in understanding new commands in less than five repetitions; statistics show that they obey a first command more than 95 percent of the time.

Border Collies have also been used in tracking, search and rescue, and Schutzhund (protection-dog) work. During World War II, a famous Border Collie named Jigger had a number of military accomplishments. His contribution to the war effort was so valued that he was given a military funeral upon his death.

The breed has enjoyed many moments in the spotlight, thanks to big-screen stardom. A Border Collie named Mike starred in the movie *Down and Out in Beverly Hills* as a dog named Matisse. The movie *Babe* showcases a talking pig that learns the ways of the world from a wise Border Collie named Fly; this hit movie was nominated for multiple Academy Awards in 1996, including Best Picture.

Other big- and small-screen Border Collie stars include:

- Chuck, from the 1984 movie *Up the Creek*
- Bandit, the Ingalls family's dog from the *Little House on the Prairie* TV series
- Gin, the dancing Border Collie from the televised talent competition *Britain's Got Talent*
- Venus, the Border Collie from Animal Planet's *Superfetch*
- Striker, the current Guinness World Record holder for "Fastest Car Window Opened by Dog" at 11.34 seconds
- Ryder, who played Judge in the 2009 film *My Sister's Keeper*

Since ancient Roman times, Border Collies and their ancestors have captured humans' attention, thanks to their intelligence, agility, and unique talents. No doubt that these dogs will continue to help us and challenge us—and delight us!

In 1940, the North American Sheep Dog Society (NASDS) began as the first sheepdog registry in the United States. Formed to protect the Border Collie and to hold sheepdog trials, the organization had a certification program for dogs based on their working ability. Several other American Border Collie organizations were formed after 1940, including these registries and clubs:

- **American Border Collie Association (ABCA):** Formed in the early 1980s, the ABCA is a registry that stresses the importance of maintaining the working ability of the breed. Those wishing to register their dogs must first become members of the association, and all dogs must meet certain criteria to be eligible for membership. The ABCA also has a Register of Merit program and promotes stockdog events.
- **Border Collie Society of America (BCSA):** The BCSA, incorporated in 1993, is a club, not a registry. This group advocates breeding Border Collies for their working abilities and promotes responsible ownership, education, and mutual support among its membership. It is the American Kennel Club's parent club for the Border Collie and is the group responsible for writing and maintaining the AKC breed standard.
- **United States Border Collie Club (USBCC):** The USBCC was founded in 1975. The club promotes the welfare of Border Collies and the preservation of the breed as a sound working dog. Members are involved in a variety of activities with their dogs, including herding and obedience.

In addition to these national and international clubs and registries, you can find club affiliates and local chapters of clubs just about everywhere. Dedicated to perpetuating and celebrating the breed, club members can be tremendous sources of information and can help you find outlets to keep your pup's boundless energy in check.

Preserving the Border Collie's working heritage is important to many breed enthusiasts.

That's One Stud

Today's Border Collies trace their lineage back to a single dog: Old Hemp. Born in 1893, Old Hemp was bred by Adam Telfer of Northumberland, England. The dog became a sensation when he hit the sheepdog-trial circuit at a year old—and never looked back.

Old Hemp stood about 21 inches tall and weighed 45 pounds. He was black and white with a long, straight coat and semi-erect ears. He is the dog who inspired today's American Kennel Club breed standard.

Boasting an unbeaten record never matched by another dog, Old Hemp wowed dog fanciers with his spectacular speed and silent yet intense style. He could cover an entire trial course in minutes without exciting the sheep. At the same time, he would keep the beasts hypnotized with his intense gaze, described by spectators as "the eye." This intense gaze that lulled sheep under his control is a characteristic today in all of his descendents.

Hemp's sire was an easygoing yet hardworking dog named Roy; his dam was named Meg, and she had such an intense eye that she had a tendency to hypnotize herself instead of the sheep, making her a near-worthless herding dog. But Old Hemp took on the positive traits of his parents, leaving the bad behind.

As a result of his sheepdog-trial successes, Old Hemp was a hot commodity. Breeders sought him as a stud dog and in his lifetime, he sired well over 200 sons and countless daughters. His progeny proved to be superior workers just like he was, and they were equally sought after by individuals around the globe.

BORDER COLLIE

W hether you're considering a Border Collie to herd your sheep, hike with you on your favorite trails, or compete in obedience or agility trials, this workaholic of the dog world will bring action and excitement to your life. The Border Collie's intelligence and trainability sets the breed apart from the rest of the pack.

Before you commit to a lifetime of caring for a Border Collie, make certain that you can provide everything that the dog needs to be happy. Border Collies need lots of challenging exercise, lots of brain-teasing activities, and lots of attention to keep their brilliant minds and energetic bodies occupied. If you don't have the time or space to dedicate to training your Border Collie and giving him work to do—either in his bred-for capacity of herding or in other suitable tasks and activities—you'll do better to consider another breed.

However, if you know this is the breed for you, the next step is finding your perfect match. This chapter will discuss how

The Border Collie is the American Kennel Club's 139th recognized breed and a member of the Herding Group. The breed placed forty-seventh in registration numbers with the AKC in 2009. That ranking climbed significantly in the decade prior—in 2000, the breed ranked sixty-fourth.

it's a **Fact**

to find a breeder and choose a healthy puppy, or, if you're considering a adopting a rescue Border Collie, where to find your newest family member.

PUPPY FEVER

Raising a puppy to adulthood is one of the most rewarding experiences you can imagine. Not only will you and your family watch and guide the puppy as he grows and develops into a bright, active, healthy adult but you'll also be able to train him for whatever work, sports, and activities you want to do with him. You can look forward to a lifetime of companionship and loyalty from your Border Collie.

You can find purebred puppies from many sources, but a reputable breeder is the best choice. How do you know that a breeder is reputable? How can you be sure that the breeder's puppies are healthy, have been bred from quality parents, and have begun to be socialized? How do you know that your Border Collie will be of sound temperament and will possess the breed's trademark intelligence, ability, and work ethic?

In your search for a quality Border Collie, start by finding several upstanding breed-

ers who have established reputations in the breed, who employ selective breeding methods, and who lovingly prepare their puppies for good homes. Reputable dog breeders are people who seek to preserve and improve their chosen breed. Often, such breeders stick to rearing one type of dog. They should be actively involved in the dog fancy, enter their dogs in herding trials or other competitive events, and show their dogs in conformation competitions. Their goal is to perfect the traits that make the Border Collie unique.

A reputable breeder chooses breeding stock very carefully, using the breed standard as a guide to produce the best puppies possible, with the goal of improving and preserving the breed's herding characteristics in each generation. Responsible breeders test their dogs for congenital defects and illnesses, and provide buyers with documentation of health screenings, a sales contract, plenty of references, and advice as needed throughout the life of the dog.

Good breeders typically do not advertise in local newspapers or online. Reputable breeders don't need to advertise in this manner because there is usually a waiting list for their healthy, well-mannered puppies. The breeder you choose should willingly open his or her home so you can inspect the facilities. The breeder should introduce you to the dam (mother) and her litter and will show you photos, pedigrees, and health certificates from the litter's sire (father) if he is not on the premises.

You can expect a good breeder to ask you about your home, your lifestyle, your experience with dogs, your knowledge of the breed, and your goals for the puppy; you may even have to complete an application. If the breeder agrees to sell you a puppy, but the arrangement doesn't work

Did You Know?

Herding trials and dog shows offer excellent opportunities to meet Border Collies in person and chat with breeders and handlers. After watching the dogs compete, talk to some of the people showing their dogs and ask them about their breeding programs or where they got their dogs.

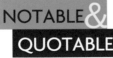

NOTABLE & QUOTABLE

You should always ask breeders how they have socialized the puppies. Have they been around other dogs? Other people? Socialization is critical in puppies from six to sixteen weeks old. Proper socialization consists of a puppy's good experiences with other puppies and different types of people.

—Debra Primovic, a veterinarian and Border Collie fan from St. Louis, Missouri

out, the breeder should be willing to take the dog back if you are no longer able to care for him.

When you find a breeder with whom you feel comfortable, ask him or her some questions—in fact, the breeder will expect you to do so! If a breeder seems put out or taken aback by your questions, it should raise a red flag.

- How long have you been breeding dogs? The more experience, the better.
- How long have you been breeding Border Collies? Do you breed other dogs? People who breed one particular type of dog are truly dedicated to bettering the breed. People who breed based on the latest fads may be of questionable character, and those who raise several different

breeds may not be able to give all of the dogs the care that they need.

- What breed and/or dog organizations do you belong to? Breeders should belong to at least one member-based club or organization, such as the Border Collie Society of America or the American Border Collie Association, with the goal of continuing their education.
- What health problems do you screen for? What congenital defects are common in Border Collies, and what are you doing to decrease those defects in your breeding program? If the breeder says, "None" or "My dogs are perfect," run the other way! All breeds have the potential for certain genetic defects, and your breeder should be honest about health problems that may present themselves in your dog's future. Do your research in advance so that you know how the breeder should answer.
- What kind of health guarantee do you offer with your dogs? At the very least, the breeder should guarantee against any debilitating health problems and congenital defects, offering a refund or a replacement puppy if such problems occur within a given time frame.
- Can I visit your facility and meet the dam? The answer to this question should always be "Of course." Even if the breeder has no puppies at the time, he or she should welcome you into the facility so you can see the dogs in the breeding program.
- What are the parents' strengths? What shortcomings do they have? Though most breeders will boast about the quality of their dams and sires, ask questions to learn about any behavioral or temperament problems, like possible aggression or poor social skills.

Did You Know?

When considering your perfect Border Collie match, sex matters. Physically, males and females differ very little, with males being slightly larger than females. Behaviorally, however, each sex embodies distinct characteristics. Males tend to maintain a constant mood, can be prone to escapism to search for females in heat (if not neutered), will mark their territory, and can challenge and disobey their handlers. Females tend to dote on their canine and human families, can be moody and temperamental, and (if not spayed) need to be sequestered from male suitors twice a year during their heat cycles.

Watching the pups interact with one or both of their parents lets you see the pups' personalities emerge as well as get a look at the breeder's adult dogs.

Questions to Expect
Be prepared for the breeder to ask you some questions, too.

1. Have you previously owned a Border Collie?

The breeder is trying to gauge how familiar you are with the Border Collie. If you have never owned one, illustrate your knowledge of the breed by telling the breeder about your research.

2. Do you have children? What are their ages?

Some breeders are wary about selling a puppy to families with younger children.

This isn't a steadfast rule, and some breeders insist on meeting the kids to see how they handle puppies. It all depends on the breeder.

3. How long have you wanted a Border Collie?

This helps a breeder know if your purchase is an impulse buy or a carefully thought-out decision. Buying on impulse is one of the biggest mistakes owners can make. Be patient.

Join Club Border to get a complete list of questions that a breeder should ask you. Click on "Downloads" at **DogChannel.com/Club-Border.**

- Where do you raise your puppies? How have you socialized them? Ideally, the breeder has raised the puppies inside the home amid the activities and sounds of normal daily activities. You want to find out whether the pups are getting used to being around people and are getting enough attention and interaction.
- How many litters do you raise each year? Breeders who produce more than three litters per year may not be paying enough attention to their dogs' health and raising the puppies. Avoid breeders who always have puppies, as that can signal irresponsible breeding practices.
- When can I take the puppy home? A reputable breeder lets puppies go to new homes when they're nine to twelve weeks old.
- Do you have a USDA license? Quality breeders are licensed by the United States Department of Agriculture, showing that their breeding facilities are safe and sanitary.

You can find breeders listed in one of the many dog-breed magazines or from an online search, but your best bet is to

A Perfect Match

Although Border Collies are known for wrangling sheep and cattle, Suzanne Heller dreamed of finding a Border Collie that could help her drive her three horses from one pasture to the other. Her dreams came true when she met Pudger, a two-year-old black-and-white Border Collie, through her local Border Collie rescue organization.

"I thought I wanted a puppy," Heller said, "but when I met Pudger, I fell in love. He was already house-trained, he wasn't chewing things anymore, and he took to moving those horses without me even training him."

Hundreds of adult Border Collies, like Pudger, wait for forever homes. Before going straight to a breeder for a puppy, think about whether an adult rescue dog could be right for you. Contact your local or national breed club for information.

locate your local or regional kennel club or Border Collie organization and ask for a list of breeder referrals. A reputable breeder, referred to you by a trusted source, is the best way to find your Border Collie puppy. If you're still not convinced, consider the following:

- While you may find a reputable backyard breeder who is learning the trade from an experienced mentor, there are backyard breeders who breed and raise purebred puppies as a commodity and have little or no interest in the dogs' well-being.
- When you acquire a Border Collie puppy from a friend's or neighbor's litter, you may know where the pup came from, but you won't necessarily know much about his background, herding instincts, or genetic health.
- You may find advertisements for puppies in newspapers and magazines, but anyone can place such an ad. If you choose to reply to one of these ads, do so with caution. Ask the same questions that you would ask a breeder who was referred to you by another Border Collie owner or a breed/dog club. Remember that cold-calling breeders is the riskiest way to find a pet.

The bottom line is that you should obtain your Border Collie puppy from someone you trust. That way, you'll know for certain where the dog came from, who his parents are, what he's been tested for, and what his potential is.

THE PICK OF THE LITTER

Once you've decided on a breeder, you'll work with the breeder to choose the right puppy for you. Of course, you should choose a puppy who's physically and mentally healthy. You want your Border Collie to begin his life with you as a sound, well-adjusted pet without obvious physical or behavioral flaws.

Begin by observing the litter at the breeder's home. Watch the puppies in a group. They should all be active and playful. There should be no sick or weak puppies in the bunch; if one is sick, the others will likely come down with the same illness.

The pups should all have clear, bright eyes with no redness or discharge; cool, damp noses; and clean ears with no signs of ear mites. None should be shaking his head or scratching at his ears, because this could indicate an ear infection. Similarly, there should be no odor from the pups' ears. Their gums should be pink and healthy. Their coats should be shiny and clean, and their skin should appear pink and healthy with no hot spots or sores. Their bodies should appear full, firm, and muscular, but their bellies should not be bloated, as this could be a sign of worms.

Before you set your sights on one puppy, watch how the littermates interact with one another and how they respond to you. Keep your eye out for an alert young Border Collie who leaps up to see you, wagging his little tail in sheer ecstasy. Avoid a pup that appears overly aggressive or domineering, charging over his littermates to get close to you or nipping at your fingers. At the other end of the spectrum, you don't want a shy, submissive pup who hides in the corner or appears listless. Stick with a dog who falls in the middle: excited but not giddy, laid-back but not listless.

With the breeder's OK, take your preferred puppy into another room or an area where he hasn't been before and do a few temperament-test exercises, which will help you assess your potential puppy's dominance, independence, and fearfulness. The exercises in a typical temperament test check a dog's willingness to react to an owner's call or follow his owner; reactions to dominance behavior, such as being rolled over or restrained; reactions to fearful situations, such as loud noises; predatory instincts, including the desire to chase or retrieve; and reactions to surprising or unexpected actions, such as an umbrella being opened. You can do a few of these simple exercises with your chosen puppy.

Gently place the puppy on the ground and watch his reaction. If he follows you, he's eager to please. If he chooses to explore his surroundings, he's a curious pup who may have a short attention span. Roll him on his back and handle his toes. If he submits, he'll respect your authority from the outset; if he squirms, he may be more challenging to train. See how the puppy reacts to loud noises and rapid movements. A Border Collie with a sound temperament will be alert, responsive, energetic, and confident.

Most breeders allow prospective pet parents to spend time with the puppies after they're five or six weeks old and take them home when they're nine to twelve weeks old, so once you pick your puppy, you can go back and visit him while he's still living with the breeder. Get to know the pup's personality before he comes home with you so there will be a seamless transition to his permanent home.

Breeder Q&A

Here are some questions you should ask a breeder and the answers you want.

Q. How often do you have litters available?

A. You want to hear "once or twice a year" or "occasionally" because a breeder who doesn't have litters that often is probably more concerned with the quality of his or her puppies than with making money.

Q. What kinds of health problems do Border Collies have?

A. Beware of a breeder who says "None." In Border Collies, some genetic health problems include hip dysplasia, osteochondritis dissecans, and various eye diseases.

Get a complete list of questions to ask a Border Collie breeder—and the ideal answers—at Club Border. Log on to **DogChannel.com/Club-Border** and click on "Downloads."

DON'T FORGET THE PAPERWORK

When homecoming day for your Border Collie arrives, the breeder will give you a packet of paperwork. It will contain all of the pertinent information on your puppy as well as advice on how to care for him. It should include:

- **Health records:** These are the puppy's complete veterinary records, including date of birth, any vaccinations he's had, any treatments he's received, and the results of any health testing he's had done. Bring these documents to your veterinarian for your pup's first checkup.
- **Care instructions:** The breeder should provide some basic advice on feeding and caring for the puppy. Often, the breeder will give details about the puppy's diet and guidance on how to groom, socialize, and house-train him.
- **Contract:** A contract is a record of the purchase of the puppy. It should list the breeder's name, the dog's name, the purchase price, the health guarantee, any spay/neuter requirements, and what to do if you can't care for the pup or dog anymore.

- **Pedigree:** This is the puppy's family tree. It should go back at least three generations and also include any titles or championships that the pup's predecessors have earned in competition.
- **Registration papers:** If your breeder's litter is registered with one of the purebred dog registries, such as the American Kennel Club or the United Kennel Club, or a Border Collie registry, such as the American Border Collie Association, the breeder should include the paperwork required to transfer the dog into your name. Registration requirements and procedures vary slightly from registry to registry, but your breeder can help you through the process.

A good breeder will also be available to you as a resource as you raise and live with your Border Collie, and that kind of resource will prove invaluable if (or when!) you have questions.

A NEW LEASH ON LIFE

As is the case with most breeds, you can find scores—if not hundreds—of Border Collies looking for new forever homes. An adult dog makes an excellent choice for a family who wants a dog but doesn't want to take on the time-consuming responsibilities of puppyhood, such as house-training and obedience classes.

You can find adult Border Collies through breed clubs and breeders. You can also find adult Border Collies through rescue organizations that specialize in finding homes for dogs whose owners can't care for them anymore; some rescue organizations are breed-specific, while others help dogs of all breeds and mixes.

Border Collie breeders can be an excellent source for finding adoptable adult dogs. Many times, a breeder may have an adult male or female who is no longer used for breeding or who no longer competes in conformation shows. A breeder may also have an adult dog who was returned because the dog's owners were no longer able to care for him. If adopting an adult from a breeder, assess the breeder just as

An adult Border Collie in need of a new home may be just the perfect match for you and your lifestyle.

you would if you were buying a puppy: ask questions, visit the facility, and check references. Expect the breeder likewise to evaluate you.

Dog rescue has become quite popular as the number of dogs euthanized in shelters has increased. Sponsored by breed clubs and independent organizations, rescue groups take in dogs from shelters and dogs who have been surrendered by their owners, and they find new homes for them.

You can find a Border Collie rescue group in your area by contacting a national breed club or rescue organization, or you can check with your humane society, animal control facility, or veterinarian for rescue information. Many of them work with rescues and can provide contact information.

Most rescues require that you fill out an application, complete an interview, and receive a home visit from a representative of the organization, who will ask you questions similar to those a breeder would ask.

When you're approved for an adoption, you'll either meet the available dogs to see if one is a good match or you'll be placed on a waiting list until a suitable adoptee for your home comes into the rescue.

The amount of background information available on a rescue dog will vary depending on how the dog came to be in rescue, but you can find out if the dog is healthy and how much training he needs. Most rescue organizations house their dogs in foster homes where they live with volunteer families while awaiting adoption, so the foster parents will be able to tell you what they've observed about the dog's personality and training.

After the dog goes home with you, the organization will follow up to be sure that the dog is settling in and that everything is working out. The group doesn't want the dog to end up back in rescue, so it takes every care to make sure that the adoption will be successful.

Healthy Puppy Signs

Here are a few things you should look for when selecting a puppy from a litter.

1. **NOSE:** It should be slightly moist to the touch, but there shouldn't be excessive discharge. The puppy should not be sneezing or sniffling persistently.

2. **SKIN AND COAT:** Your Border Collie puppy's coat should be soft and shiny, without flakes or excessive shedding. Watch out for patches of missing hair, redness, bumps, or sores. The pup should have a pleasant smell. Check for parasites, such as fleas or ticks.

3. **BEHAVIOR:** A healthy Border Collie puppy may be sleepy, but he should not be lethargic. A healthy puppy will be playful at times, not isolated in a corner. You should see occasional bursts of energy and interaction with his littermates. When it's mealtime, a healthy puppy will take an interest in his food.

There are other signs to look for when picking out the perfect puppy for your lifestyle. Download the list at **DogChannel.com/Club-Border.**

NOTABLE & QUOTABLE *Whether selecting your prospective pup from a professional breeder or from [someone who is] breeding a litter for the very first time, the criteria are the same: look for puppies who have been raised indoors around human companionship and influence, around people who have devoted lots of time to the puppies' education.*

—Ian Dunbar, veterinarian and animal behaviorist who runs Sirius Puppy Training in the San Francisco Bay area

You've found the Border Collie for you and, ready or not, here he comes! Before his homecoming, you'll need to do some careful planning to make sure that your home is ready and that all his needs will be met. From putting away puppy temptations and securing the yard to choosing nutritious food and buying boredom-busting toys, your dog relies on you for his well-being and survival. Clean up, stock up, and prepare in advance, because the time to do it is before—not after—your pup arrives.

Besides puppy-proofing and supply shopping, you'll also want to plan how to introduce your new Border Collie to the entire family, including other furry, feathered, or finned creatures. Children in the house will need to learn how to live with a herding dog, while cats, small animals, and other critters will need special one-on-one introductions under your watchful eye.

Dog services and supplies aren't cheap. According to the American Pet Products Association's 2011–2012 National Pet Owners Survey, in 2010, dog owners spent an average of $407 per year for their dogs' surgical veterinary care, $274 for boarding, $254 for food, $248 for routine vet visits, and $78 for travel expenses. On the low end, dog owners spent a yearly average of $17 on leashes and $42 on standard collars.

it's a **Fact**

In this chapter, we'll explain how to give your Border Collie a smooth transition into your home. Whether you're bringing home a twelve-week-old puppy or an adult rescue, remember that the dog is entering a brand-new world, and he'll appreciate your love—and patience—as he makes it through his first nights in his new home.

SAFE HOME, SAFE DOG

When puppy-proofing your home and yard, put all temptations and valuables well out of your Border Collie's reach—for his safety and your sanity. This clever dog will explore his environment and investigate everything, and he won't make the distinction between your favorite pair of shoes and his chew toy. To prepare your home and yard for your new dog, get on all fours and look at the world from his perspective, which is about 2 feet off the ground. The first item on your to-do list is to remove any potential dangers from each room of your house and your yard before your Border Collie comes home.

Kitchen

The kitchen contains all sorts of interesting drawers, cabinets, and cords, not to mention smells and tastes. If he can get into a cabinet or drawer, your Border Collie will want to inspect everything inside. Childproof latches, found at your local hardware store, prevent curious dogs from opening cabinets and drawers. As an added precaution, keep food and any cleaning supplies or other household chemicals out of the dog's reach.

Power cords look like fun chew toys to a teething Border Collie but can be very dangerous if he sinks his teeth into them. Tucking cords and wires out of reach, blocking them, or enclosing them in chew-proof PVC tubing will keep them intact and keep your dog safe.

Tempting smells will entice your Border Collie, too, so be diligent about putting leftovers away rather than leaving them out on the counter. Secure the garbage can with a locking lid or store it behind a latched cabinet door to keep the rubbish inside the can, not all over the kitchen floor (or inside your Border Collie's belly)!

Bathroom

The bathroom can be a dangerous place for a dog. Razors, pills, cotton swabs, and soap left within your dog's reach can be easily ingested, which can mean an emergency visit to your veterinarian. Family members need to be conscientious about cleaning up after themselves in the bathroom. Put shampoos, soap, tissues, and accessories out of reach or inside a cabinet or drawer. Especially while your Border Collie is young, always keep the toilet lid down. A curious pup could jump into the bowl and drown. Use a wastebasket with a locking lid, or stash it in a cabinet under the sink. Install childproof latches on the drawers and cabinets, and be sure to tuck dangling cords away, out of your dog's reach. Even with all of these safety precautions, make it a habit to keep the bathroom door closed.

Did You Know?

Americans—and a lot of them— love their dogs. According to the American Pet Products Association's 2011–2012 Annual Pet Owners Survey, 46.3 million U.S. households owned dogs in 2010, up from 34.1 million in 1988.

Your curious, on-the-go Border Collie pup will need a dog-proof home indoors and out and your supervision.

Bedroom

Dogs are scent-oriented, so they gravitate toward anything that smells like you. Shoes, slippers, and clothing will become toys if you don't safeguard such items behind closed closet doors or in drawers. Keep clothing off the floor, store shoes out of reach, and put laundry in a tall hamper with a lid.

Store jewelry, hair ties, coins, and other small ingestible items in containers or drawers, and secure any exposed cords or wires. Many dogs like to curl up under the bed or wedge themselves behind furniture, so put up temporary blockades to prevent

Border Collies, like all other dogs, are creatures of habit. They prefer to rise at the same time every morning and have regular potty breaks, regular meals, regular work hours, and regular playtime. When your puppy or new dog comes home, have your dog's routine planned in advance and make sure that all of the family members know their roles. Doing so will make life with your Border Collie easier for everyone.

your Border Collie from hiding where he shouldn't be hiding.

Kids' rooms contain all kinds of fun Border Collie treasures, like tyke-sized shoes and clothing, plush toys, blocks, school supplies—all of which look like toys to a dog. Remind your children to pick up after themselves and to keep their belongings out of the puppy's reach.

Office

Your Border Collie may be drawn to all sorts of temptations in your office, like papers, magazines, cords and wires, paper clips, rubber bands, and staples. These items may be fun for your dog to play with, but they can be fatal if chewed or swallowed. As with the rest of the house, pick up strewn office supplies and store them in a desk drawer, secure or enclose cords and wires, and keep decorative items well out of your Border Collie's reach.

Garage and Yard

When you look around your garage and yard, you'll see many obvious and not-so-obvious dangers to your Border Collie. Paint, cleaners, insecticides, fertilizers,

antifreeze, and gasoline represent a handful of poisons and chemicals that you may have in your garage or outdoor shed. Rat poisons, snail bait, and ant traps can look like toys or tasty treats to your pet. Secure all such substances in a locked cabinet or store them on high shelves that your dog can't reach.

Border Collies are curious dogs, and they'll investigate—and possibly dig up—many of the plants in your yard if left unattended. Some plants, such as daffodils, foxgloves, birds of paradise, and lupines can be poisonous to your dog. Toxic plants cause varied reactions, including rashes, vomiting, and diarrhea; some can even be fatal. You can find a list of the most commonly encountered toxic plants at the American Society for the Prevention of Cruelty to Animals' (ASPCA) website: www.aspca.org. Their Animal Poison Control Center page can be found under "Pet Care." The ASPCA offers information online and also hosts a poison-control hotline that owners can call for a fee in emergency situations. Protect your pup—and your foliage—by fencing in plants and blocking access to off-limits areas of the yard and garden.

Power tools and gardening equipment should also be kept out of your Border Collie's reach. Sniffing a sharp blade could cut his delicate nose, or tugging on a cord may cause a heavy saw to fall and break one of his bones, or worse.

SHOPPING FOR SUPPLIES

Once your house is prepared for your new Border Collie, the next task on your to-do list is to purchase some gear. You can find doggy supplies at independent pet-supply stores, pet-supply superstores, supermarkets, and discount stores. Let's go shopping!

Many items that you use in your home and yard can be toxic to dogs, causing rashes, vomiting, diarrhea, or worse. As you're puppy-proofing your home, put these products out of your Border Collie's reach:

- Acetaminophen
- Antifreeze
- Bleach
- Boric acid
- Car fluids
- Cleaning products
- Deodorizers
- Detergents
- Disinfectants
- Drain cleaners
- Furniture polish
- Gasoline
- Herbicides
- Insect sprays, baits, and traps
- Kerosene
- Matches
- Medications
- Moth balls
- Nail polish and remover
- Paint
- Rat poison
- Rubbing alcohol
- Turpentine

Collar and Leash

Your Border Collie will need a collar and leash right away. Available in a range of colors and materials, the collar is necessary for attaching your dog's leash and holding his license tag and ID tag, which lists your contact information should he ever get lost. For a puppy, pick up an adjustable nylon collar with a buckle. Find the right size by measuring the diameter of your Border Collie's neck and adding 2 inches for growing room; you can expand the collar as he grows.

The leash gives you control of your Border Collie during walks and training. When you purchase a leash, make sure that it latches securely to the collar and is comfortable to hold. For a puppy's first leash, a 4- to 6-foot nylon or cotton variety is all you'll need.

ID, Please

Providing your dog with proper identification is the only way to increase the odds that you and your Border Collie will be reunited if you somehow get separated. Readily visible on your dog's collar, an ID tag typically lists your dog's name and your name, address, and telephone number. At the very least, it should list your name and the best way to contact you.

A microchip is an additional method of identifying your Border Collie. Injected by your veterinarian under the skin between your dog's shoulder blades, this is a tiny device that contains a code that is stored in a database with your contact information. Many animal shelters, veterinarians' offices, and even police stations are equipped with handheld scanners that can read the code in the microchip. The code is then entered into the database, which brings up your name and phone number so that you can be contacted, and you and your dog can be reunited.

If you microchip your dog, take the time to register your information with the database and keep it up to date. The microchip won't do any good if there's no name or phone number associated with it or if the information is incorrect. Similarly, if you rehome your dog, notify the registry and have the new owners update it as necessary.

Bowl Basics

Your Border Collie will need two sets of food and water bowls when he comes home; you'll need a spare in case one set is in the dishwasher. They generally come in plastic, ceramic, and stainless-steel versions; choose what fits your budget, but keep in mind that while plastic can harbor bacteria and ceramic can break, stainless steel can be sanitized and is virtually indestructible. With a young puppy, you can get away with a 16- or 24-ounce standard-depth bowl, but plan to purchase larger bowls as the pup's food intake increases.

Diet Delights

Before you bring your Border Collie home, purchase dog food and some healthy treats. Whether you're bringing a puppy home from a breeder or adopting an adult dog from a rescue organization, find out what kind of canine cuisine the dog has been eating. For healthy development, puppies need a diet formulated for growth; your breeder can recommend a good puppy formula as well as what kind of adult food to switch to as your Border Collie matures. Healthy adults simply need a diet formulated for maintenance. (Turn to chapter 8 for more information on nutrition and feeding.)

Crates, Pens, and Gates

A must for any puppy owner, crates and exercise pens ("X-pens") keep your Border Collie safe in a confined area where you can monitor him, train him, and transport him.

Your pup's crate serves as a house-training tool, a cozy dog den, and a safe place for him to relax when strangers come to visit. Crates come in a variety of materials, including plastic, fiberglass, powder-coated wire, and stainless steel. The hard-sided plastic and fiberglass models frequently double as airline-approved carriers (check with your airline to be certain). When choosing a crate, be mindful of size. Select a crate that will allow your Border Collie to be comfortable when fully grown, but make sure that it includes a divider so you can create a puppy-sized area for your youngster. A too-large crate will not provide the proper den-like environment for your pup.

An X-pen is a portable wire pen that confines your pup to a specific area. The pen's adjustable panels can be arranged to fit spaces of different sizes and shapes. You can enclose your pup, his crate, his food and water bowls, and some toys inside the pen.

Baby gates give your Border Collie a little more freedom in the house by blocking doorways to confine your pup to one room or part of the house, keeping the rest off limits. Some can be permanently installed in door frames, while others are pressure mounted and can be removed whenever you want.

A Cozy Bed

Everyone, your dog included, loves a comfy bed. You'll want to give your Border Collie a soft place to lay his head starting with his first night home. Because you'll be house-training and crate-training your puppy, your pup's first bed should be something that fits inside his crate and is easily washable, such as a crate pad or an old blanket. After he's house-trained, you can choose an appropriately sized dog bed that your Border Collie can use outside his crate.

Toys, Toys, and More Toys

Border Collies love their toys. When they're not working, these crafty canines need something to keep them busy, and toys help do just that. Different toys serve different purposes: some are built to be chewed, some are intended to provide comfort, and others are designed to challenge the brain and encourage problem solving. Before you go shopping, ask your breeder or the rescue volunteers if your Border Collie prefers certain types of toys. When giving him new toys, offer them one at a time so that he's not overwhelmed by too many choices. It won't take long to discover what your dog fancies.

Clean-Up Duty

Cleaning up after your dog is one of the necessary evils of pet ownership. Before your Border Collie comes home, invest in a poop scoop or other similar device to make the chore easier. You should also pick up some clean-up bags for walks around the neighborhood or in any public places. To clean up indoor potty accidents, get an enzyme-based cleaner that's designed to neutralize the odors and thus prevent your dog from relieving himself again in the same spot.

Grooming Goods

To care for your Border Collie's coat, you'll need some supplies. For a puppy, you won't need too much: a soft brush, shampoo formulated for puppies, a small doggy toothbrush and doggy toothpaste, and some small nail trimmers. As your pup grows, or if you're bringing home an adult, you'll need more advanced grooming supplies, including shampoo and conditioner formulated for adult coats, a hair dryer made for dogs, a quality comb with narrowly spaced teeth on one end and wider set teeth on the other, slicker and bristle brushes, a grooming rake for removing mats, heavier duty nail clippers, and more. (See chapter 9.)

MEETING THE PACK

When your Border Collie finally comes home, give him the opportunity to explore his new home, and introduce him to the other members of the pack, including children and other pets. Your new puppy or adult Border Collie will integrate into the family smoothly if you set up proper greetings and encourage him with positive reinforcement and praise.

A Tour of the House

Though you may be tempted to let your Border Collie check out his new surroundings on his own, you shouldn't give him free rein right away. Instead, take him from room to room and give him a little time to become familiar with each new area. Show him his designated area, which can be one dog-proofed room or an area where his crate is located. Point out his food and water bowls, and take him to his potty area outside. As time goes on and you feel more confident about your Border Collie's behavior and house-training, you can give him more freedom to explore on his own.

Kids, Meet Pup

If you have children, or if kids frequent your home, they're probably more excited about your Border Collie than you are! Most kids adore puppies, but a young person's exuberant behavior could be a bit much for your new dog. Children who are awkward or inexperienced around animals could unintentionally hurt or startle a puppy or dog.

When introducing a child to the dog, try the following step-by-step technique to prevent either of them from becoming overstimulated or accidentally injured:

1. Sit on the floor or in a chair and hold the puppy in your arms or have the adult dog next to you. Ask the child to approach slowly, not moving too quickly or erratically.
2. Invite the child to pet the dog gently. Demonstrate how to handle a dog with

Monitor the condition of all of your pup's toys to ensure that they're intact and safe for chewing.

Some ordinary household items make great toys for your Border Collie—as long you make sure that they are safe. Tennis balls, plastic water bottles, old towels, and more can be transformed into fun with a little creativity. You can find a list of homemade toys at **DogChannel.com/Club-Border.**

In most counties and states, licensing your dog is the law. To apply for a dog license, contact the proper agency in your town or city, usually either the health department or animal control division. You will fill out a form with your name, address, and phone number, as well as your pet's name, breed, sex, age, microchip number (if applicable), and whether your dog has been spayed or neutered. You will also have to provide proof of a rabies vaccination. Upon approval, you will receive a licensing tag with a unique number that should be attached to your dog's collar. Licensing fees vary, but generally, unaltered animals cost more to license than spayed or neutered animals. Renewal forms are sent out annually.

care, modeling the behavior and allowing the child to mimic you. Point out the puppy's eyes, nose, and mouth; let the child know that these are sensitive, off-limit areas on the dog's body.

3. If you have a puppy, and the child asks to hold the puppy, have the child sit on the floor. Gently place the pup in the child's lap. Tell him or her to handle and touch the puppy gently. Don't let the child hold the puppy too tightly.

4. Watch the dog's—and the child's—body language. If either starts to squirm or cry, playtime is over. Place the pup back in his crate or pen and reward him for good behavior.

5. After the Border Collie and the child have met, talk with the child about the house rules concerning the dog. Make sure that the child understands that the dog is not a toy, that he requires special handling, and that you (or another adult) must be present when the child wants to play with the dog.

As herding dogs, Border Collies will try to herd children and wrangle running boys and girls, which could inadvertently result in injury, so instruct kids not to act wild around the dog or encourage him to chase them. As the children and the puppy get older and more accustomed to each other, the more freedom they can have to play together.

Introducing Other Pets

Your Border Collie will, after some supervised introductions and positive reinforcement, get along well with other pets in your home, but it will take some time and practice. The process can be very easy or very difficult; it all depends on the personalities and temperaments of the animals.

To play it safe, put your Border Collie in his crate and bring the crate to the other pet. Let them look at each other and sniff each other. Watch their body language. Is the cat hissing or curious? Is the dog growling, or is he wagging his tail? If they seem to get along well, let the dog out of the crate and see what both pets do, being very watchful in case a fight breaks out. The two will sniff each other some more, check each other out, and nudge each other with their noses. If you're lucky, they'll start playing and become fast friends. If the pup or the other animal shows no interest in the other, don't force it; they'll interact when they're ready.

When you bring two dogs together, keep in mind that the current dog may see the newcomer as a threat to his place in the pack, depending on the resident dog's

Once your Border Collie is crate-trained, **he will be comfortable in his** crate **both inside** your home and wherever **you** go.

NOTABLE & QUOTABLE

The more you confine your puppy to his crate and X-pen during the first few weeks at home, the more freedom he will enjoy as an adult dog for the rest of his life. If you do [crate him], the sooner your puppy will be house-trained and chew-toy trained. And, as an added benefit, your puppy will learn to settle down quickly, quietly, calmly, and happily.

—Ian Dunbar, a veterinarian and animal behaviorist who runs Sirius Puppy Training in the San Francisco Bay area

temperament and personality. Introduce them in a neutral environment, someplace other than your house or yard (a.k.a. the current dog's "turf"). Watch their behavior, and if the current dog begins to display dominant or aggressive behavior, separate them and try again later. After several meetings, they'll learn to live with each other.

If you're introducing your Border Collie to your cat (who will likely be a little aloof and possibly defensive), be especially cautious of the cat's claws and the dog's eyes. If a fight breaks out, your cat can scratch your dog's eyes, which are especially delicate in a puppy, requiring an emergency call to your veterinarian.

After your pets begin to get along, let them play together—always supervised, of course. After the animals recognize that the other is not a threat, they'll share the same space and become part of the same pack.

SURVIVING THE FIRST NIGHT

After a long day filled with exploring his new home and meeting his new family, your Border Collie will be bushed. No doubt you'll be ready for a good night's sleep, too. The truth is, however, that the first night with your new dog will be a long one for both of you, particularly with a puppy. Rather than cuddling with his mama and littermates,

your Border Collie youngster will be bunking all alone in an unfamiliar place with strange smells and sounds. He'll be scared, and rightfully so! As a new puppy parent, you can expect to be up throughout the night, at least for that first night.

To make it easier on everyone, plan to bring your Border Collie home when you have two full days off in a row, meaning that you'll have two full days to spend with your new dog and establish routines for eating, going to the bathroom, and playing.

On that first night, here's what to expect:

- Plenty of potty breaks: Because your pup has yet to learn to control his bladder and bowels, you'll need to take him outside to relieve himself at least every two hours. Even with an adult dog, frequent potty trips are a good idea, as you may not be sure right away how reliable he is with house-training.
- Frequent clean-ups: Even with all those potty trips, you can expect accidents. Line the crate with absorbent pads to soak up messes, and have some pet-safe cleanser and rags ready.
- Sad puppy whimpers: Heartbreaking, indeed! Your pup will be lonely and will let you know it, but resist the urge to comfort the pup. If you go to him every time he cries, you'll teach him that he gets his way when he cries—and that's a hard habit to break.

By the time the sun rises the next day, you'll be exhausted, but you will have survived the first night. If you have a puppy, you might not get uninterrupted sleep for several months until your Border Collie becomes house-trained and trustworthy, but don't worry—it will get easier, especially as your pup grows accustomed to the routine.

Though much loved by dogs, sticks can splinter when chewed, causing injury or choking.

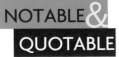

NOTABLE & QUOTABLE   *To help a puppy ease into his new home, the owners should first of all bring as many familiar objects as is practical from the previous environment, such as a blanket, some toys, or even a bed. And they should make sure that they bring some of the food that the pup is eating so he has as much continuity as possible.*

—Nicolas Dodman, veterinarian, animal behaviorist, and director of the animal behavior clinic at Tufts University's Cummings School of Veterinary Medicine in North Grafton, Massachusetts

YOUR HERDER

When you bring your new Border Collie puppy home, the first things he should learn are bladder control and when and where to go potty. This process is called house-training, and it's critical that you start your pup's training from day one. Because he typically won't eliminate in the same space where he eats and sleeps, keeping your dog in his crate or in a restricted area trains him to hold it until it's time to visit the designated bathroom area.

Because they're intelligent dogs, Border Collies are relatively easy to house-train compared to many other dogs, but keep in mind that the process will take time. Each dog is different, but a Border Collie generally can be house-trained by six to eight months old, if not sooner, as long as his

More than half of dog owners who work leave their canine companions home alone, according to the American Pet Product Association's 2011–2012 National Pet Owners Survey. Of the respondents, 54 percent said that they left their pets alone during the day; 44 percent reported that someone was at home with their dogs during the day; and the remainder relied on friends, neighbors, and doggy day care for dog-sitting duties.

it's a **Fact**

owners are consistent with a daily routine and do not force the dog to hold it for too long. Be patient, stick to a schedule, and remember to praise your pup for doing the right thing!

CRAZY FOR THE CRATE

The crate is your Border Collie's den, place to relax, and favorite napping spot. It's also a confined space where you can safely put your dog when you have to run to the store or tend to chores that demand all of your attention. Dogs, being den animals, prefer to rest in dark, close spaces, so it won't be difficult to teach your pup that his crate is a happy place.

Crates can be found at pet-supply stores or at some large general-merchandise stores. They come in stainless-steel and powder-coated wire, solid plastic or fiber-glass with peepholes and ventilation, sturdy rattan, and even flexible canvas. Some are collapsible, some are airline approved, and all are portable. Whatever type you choose, make sure that your Border Collie will have enough room to stand up, lie down, stretch out, and turn around in the crate when he reaches his adult size. Many crates come with dividers and inserts that allow the kennel to grow with the dog; a smaller area will help with house-training and make your puppy feel cozy in his den, not lost in a void of empty space.

Your Border Collie should always associate his crate with positive experiences (such as napping or chewing on his favorite toy); the crate should *never* be a place for punishment. Place the crate in an area of the house where your family hangs out, such as the kitchen or family room, so your puppy won't feel alone, and get him used to his new "bedroom" with these tips:

1. When your Border Collie comes home, introduce him to his crate by showing him his new den, tossing a treat inside, and, in an upbeat voice, issuing a verbal cue such as "Crate" or "Kennel." Ever inquisitive, your puppy is bound to go in and explore. Reward him with praise and another treat when he does, but don't close the crate door yet. Just keep repeating this action, cue, and reward process until your Border Collie associates the verbal command with the treat and, ultimately, with the praise. This may take some time, but your pup will get it if you're patient and remember to reward the desired behavior.

NOTABLE & QUOTABLE

Puppies have a forty-five-minute bladder capacity at three weeks of age, a seventy-five-minute capacity at eight weeks, a ninety-minute capacity at twelve weeks, and a two-hour capacity at eighteen weeks. Releasing your puppy every hour offers you an hourly opportunity to reward your dog for using a designated toilet area.

—Ian Dunbar, a veterinarian and animal behaviorist who runs
Sirius Puppy Training in the San Francisco Bay area

What do you do when you catch your Border Collie in the middle of having an accident? *Correct* and *redirect*. The act of going to the bathroom isn't the mistake—it's going in the wrong place. If you catch your pup in an accident, tell him "No" in a corrective tone and immediately take him out to his potty spot and let him finish his business there. Be sure to praise your pup and celebrate that he's going outside.

2. Once your pup freely enters and exits his crate without hesitation, you can begin to feed him in it. Begin by putting his bowl near the crate, associating the crate with the positive experience of eating. With each meal, move the food closer to the crate and then inside the crate. Eventually, place the food toward the back of the crate so that your Border Collie must go all the way inside to eat. Leave the door open until he is comfortable eating inside.

3. When your Border Collie will quietly go into the crate and eat his food, close the door while he eats. At first, open the door immediately after he finishes his meal, and then leave the door closed for longer and longer periods of time until he's comfortable with the door being closed for ten minutes or so.

4. If your pup cries or whines to be let out, wait until he stops fussing before you open the door, as you don't want him to associate whining with getting his way. Instead, go back to keeping the door closed for shorter stints of time and slowly work back up to longer periods.

5. Train your Border Collie to stay in his crate for longer and longer periods of time with lots of praise and treats. After a while, you'll be able to leave him in the crate for several hours at a time, which will allow you freedom to run errands while the puppy naps. The rule of thumb is to use the puppy's age in months plus one to determine the maximum amount of time in hours that he can be left in the crate; for example, a two-month-old pup can be left in his crate no longer than three hours. But remember, six hours is the limit for puppies and dogs older than six months.

6. Teach your puppy to sleep in his crate at night. Move the crate from the family room to the bedroom at night, and when it's time for bed, use your crate cue to tell the puppy to go inside. Give him lots of praise and close the crate door. Try to keep one ear open throughout the night so that you'll hear the puppy if he needs to go potty.

Before long, your Border Collie will learn that his crate is his special room. As he won't want to soil his area, he'll learn that he has to wait to go to the bathroom.

How often does a Border Collie puppy do his business? A lot! Go to DogChannel.com/Club-Border and download the typical potty schedule of a puppy. You can also download a chart that you can fill out to track your dog's elimination timetable, which will help you with house-training.

Success! House-training is a collaborative effort between dog and owner.

People think that crates are miserable for their puppies, but I explain to my students that they should look at the puppy's crate like it's the puppy's bedroom. Puppies need their own space, just like [the owners] did when they were teenagers.

—Linda White, canine acupressurist, dog trainer, and president of Happy Puppy Kindergarten, Inc., from Phoenix, Arizona

That's where crate-training and house-training go hand in hand.

HOW TO HOUSE-TRAIN

House-training involves teaching your dog to let you know when and where he needs to eliminate and how to do it on command. At first, he won't be able to signal to you that he needs to relieve himself; you'll be the one taking him out regularly and telling him when it's time to go. In time, however, your Border Collie will learn to control his bladder and bowels, let you know when he needs to go outside, and use a designated area as his potty spot.

Your puppy will be ready to start house-training when he comes home with you; in fact, your breeder may have already started the process. Plan to continue house-training until your dog is six months old, and expect to limit his freedom in the home until he's one year old. By the end of this training period, you'll have confidence that your pup knows when and where to do his business. Take comfort in knowing that the Border Collie is one of the easier breeds to house-train. Stay consistent with the following three-pronged approach: limiting his freedom, enforcing a designated potty area, and using a verbal potty cue.

Restrict His Freedom

When your Border Collie comes home, he will have little to no house-training knowledge. If you are adopting an adult, you may not know the extent of his house-training experience, but it is hoped that he at least understands the basic concept of going outside. Until your Border Collie's habits become more established and he learns how to control his bladder and bowels, you'll need to limit him to a certain area of the house.

You can restrict your Border Collie's freedom by using his crate, as previously discussed, or by containing him in an exercise pen. Because an X-pen will give your pup more space than a crate, he may choose a corner of the pen for a bathroom area. Line the entire floor surface with layers of newspaper or absorbent house-training pads to soak up any accidents, and clean the area thoroughly if (when) accidents happen.

When your puppy is outside his restricted area, he must be supervised at all times. Right after he comes back inside from a potty trip is a good time to let him play and explore with one of the family members close by, but remember to get him outside quickly if you notice any body language that indicates his need to "go."

Did You Know?

Cleaning up after your pooch is dirty business, and all sorts of devices are now available to make this task mess free. No longer is the old plastic grocery bag the receptacle of choice. You can choose from scoops, claws, and shovels, and you can buy small dispensers of waste bags that attach to your Border Collie's lead. If you really want nothing to do with cleaning up your dog's droppings, however, a pooper-scooper service can do your dirty work. Such a service sends someone to your home a number of times during the week to pick up your dog's feces for a fee. It could be a convenience to consider!

Don't allow your Border Collie to become distracted on a potty trip outdoors—it's business first!

Having house-training problems with your Border Collie? Ask other Border owners for advice and tips, or post your own success story to give other owners encouragement. Log on to **DogChannel.com/Club-Border** and click on "Community."

If your Border Collie continues to have accidents over and over in the same spot, he's following his nose. Dogs tend to sniff out the same spot in which to urinate and defecate, which is why you can train him to an area outdoors, but also why he may be tempted to revisit an indoor area in which he's soiled before. You'll need to do everything you can to remove the odor of an indoor mess. Clean the area with white vinegar or an enzyme-based pet stain cleaner, which is formulated to destroy the odor-causing bacteria found in pet waste.

Introduce the Bathroom Area

Dogs are creatures of habit. House-training will be much easier for you and your Border Collie if you designate a particular bathroom area and take your pup there frequently. When you designate a potty spot, choose an out-of-the-way area of your yard and always take your pup on leash to that same area when he has to eliminate.

When he eliminates, use a verbal cue, such as "Go potty," to help him associate a command with eliminating. Immediately after your Border relieves himself in the proper area, praise him lavishly and give him a treat. Don't wait until he comes inside to reward him—by then, it will be too late, and he won't associate the reward with the act of relieving himself. Immediately giving the dog positive reinforcement lets him know what's expected of him and what pleases you.

To teach your puppy where he shouldn't go to the bathroom, you also want to show him the other rooms in the home where he doesn't normally spend time, such as the bedrooms, guest rooms, dining room, and den. Once he recognizes these rooms as places where the family lives, he'll be less likely to use them as alternative bathroom spots when you increase his freedom.

Naptime means that potty time is soon to follow. Make a trip outdoors after your pup wakes up part of the routine.

A house-trained Border Collie is a happy Border Collie—with an equally happy owner!

Potty on Cue

Teaching your puppy to go to the bathroom on command and in the right place will challenge both of you. Don't worry, it's actually not that difficult. You (and your family) just need to be committed to consistent training, which means following the same steps every time you take your Border Collie to the bathroom. You can tweak the routine as your pup starts to get the hang of house-training.

Assuming that you've introduced your puppy to the different rooms of the house, his confined area, and his approved bathroom spot, you can follow these step-by-step instructions to guide you through the potty-training process. Remember that each family member should follow these steps consistently every time your pup needs to go out to relieve himself.

1. When it's time to go outside, say, "Outside" in a happy, upbeat tone. Attach your Border Collie's leash to his collar and lead him to the bathroom area. Plan to do this regularly throughout the day, including:
   - After he wakes up in the morning
   - After every nap
   - After he eats
   - After playtime
   - After baths
   - Before he goes to bed
   - Every two hours (or so) in addition to the above times

2. As soon as he starts eliminating, say "Go potty." He knows what he's doing, and by giving him a verbal command, he links his action with your cue. Teaching him to go on cue is particularly useful when it's raining or snowing outside, when you're running late for work, or when you're on a road trip and don't have a lot of time to spare.

3. Immediately after he's done, say "Good boy" or whatever phrase or word you choose, and give him a tasty morsel. He'll begin to make three important associations: the cue ("Go potty") with the action of eliminating, the action of eliminating with the food reward, and the food reward with your praise. You're teaching your dog that by going potty on cue, he will earn a reward. You'll eventually phase out the treats so that your praise ultimately will be his reward.

Your Border Collie will quickly show signs of grasping the house-training concept. He'll begin to wait by the door or come up with some other way to tell you, "I have to go!" He'll be able to hold his bladder throughout the night without

Did You Know?

Border Collies are brilliant, but don't assume that they can connect seemingly disparate cause-and-effect scenarios. If your dog is unsupervised in the house and has an accident, and you see the mess and correct him hours (or even minutes) later, he won't understand the connection between the mistake and the correction; corrections only work if you catch him in the act (with any undesired behavior). Instead, reward your Border Collie's correct behavior. Reinforcing the positive is the best way to discourage the negative.

Clear Signals

Sidney, a three-year-old black-and-white Border Collie, had no trouble grasping the house-training concept when his owner, Ami Frye, taught him the basics. The sharp-as-a-whip dog, who Frye adopted from a local Border Collie rescue group when he was just a three-month-old puppy, enjoyed spending time in his crate while Frye was at work. He was able to hold it until he made his way to his backyard bathroom spot. He even learned to go potty on command.

When Frye learned that dogs could be trained to tell their owners when they had to go outside by ringing a bell dangling from the doorknob, she wanted to take Sidney's training to the next level.

"It's kind of like Pavlov's dogs, where a repeated stimulus creates an expected outcome, which is to go outside," Frye says. "Sidney learned that when he nudged the bells and they made that ringing sound, I would let him outside to go to the bathroom—which was a reward in itself."

It took about ten days of training, Frye says. First, she introduced the bells to Sidney, allowing him to sniff them and ring them. Next, she hung them on the doorknob. Every time Frye and Sidney went outside, she issued the cue "Ring your bells" and had Sidney touch the bells to his nose before they exited. When he did as he was instructed, Frye rewarded him with lots of praise (and potty time).

"Consistency was key to teaching him this trick," she says, adding that her entire family followed the same routine during the training period. "Sidney is such a smart dog. We didn't even have to tempt him with treats!"

whimpering. You'll be able to let him out in the yard without his leash, and he'll head to his bathroom spot right away. It will take time—at least six months—before he gets the hang of it all, but don't worry, he will.

The key to house-training is setting your dog up to succeed and not giving him the opportunity to make a mistake. Keep him in your sight at all times, and if you see him start to walk in circles or display other signs that he's about to relieve himself, get him outside to his bathroom spot right away. When he does his business, always praise him and give him a treat. When you cannot supervise him, let him spend time in his crate or pen, and take him outside as soon as you release him.

As smart as they are, Border Collies still need help taking care of themselves, particularly when it comes to their health. As a responsible dog owner, something you'll need to do before your pup comes home is form a relationship with a veterinarian you trust—someone who knows the breed, whose office is nearby, and with whom you feel comfortable voicing questions and concerns.

Along with finding a top-notch dog doc, you'll also need to learn how to keep your Border Collie healthy at home and prevent accidents before they happen. In addition

Dogs reach sexual maturity between the ages of six to nine months old, at which time they are capable of reproducing. To prevent unwanted puppies, your veterinarian can perform a simple surgery on your Border Collie. Females are spayed; the ovaries and uterus are removed surgically. Not only does this procedure prevent unwanted puppies but it also will protect her from ovarian cancer and mammary gland cancer. Males are neutered; their testicles are removed through a small incision. Added benefits of neutering include less marking and leg lifting, less aggression, and protection from testicular cancer.

it's a
Fact

to vaccinating your pet against common diseases, you should bone up on canine first aid so you'll be prepared to manage those inevitable scrapes and bruises. With a little knowledge and common sense, caring for your dog isn't difficult, but, as a smart owner, you'll want to be prepared for anything.

VETTING YOUR VETERINARIAN

Aside from you, your dog's veterinarian will become his best friend. Besides keeping your Border Collie healthy and disease-free, your vet will conduct annual screenings and suggest preventive care to ensure that your dog will enjoy a long life of herding and play. Your vet will recommend vaccinations and booster shots as needed, treat your dog for any illness or injury that happens, prescribe medications, and be available for any questions or concerns that you may have.

You can find area veterinarians listed in your local phone directory or online, or ask dog-owning friends and family to recommend their favorites. The best referrals often come from your breeder or local Border Collie club, as they are likely to recommend doctors who are experienced with the breed and its particular ailments.

Types of Veterinarians

Like doctors for humans, veterinarians may choose to be general practitioners or specialists. Veterinarians may also choose to incorporate alternative therapies into their practices.

General practitioners can perform many of the services that your Border Collie will need, including annual checkups, vaccinations, minor surgeries, diagnostics, and preventive care. If your dog is sick, first take him to your general practitioner. Veterinarians are licensed through the American Veterinary Medical Association. If your Border Collie needs specialized care, your general practitioner will refer you to a specialist.

Veterinary specialists, such as veterinary behaviorists, surgeons, or dentists, undergo further training in their chosen disciplines. To become a veterinary specialist, the person must earn his or her veterinary degree (DVM) and then complete an internship and residency program in the chosen discipline. The certification requirements vary but are governed by the American Board of Veterinary Specialists.

In addition to traditional veterinary care, you may consider a veterinarian who offers complementary and alternative health care for your Border Collie. Some of these alternative modalities include acupuncture, acupressure, massage, and chiropractic care. Before visiting an alternative-medicine practitioner, consult your traditional veterinarian for recommendations, advice, or further information.

Beyond the License

Choosing a veterinarian with experience and credentials is important, but you should also make sure that the vet and his

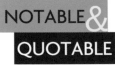

NOTABLE & QUOTABLE

You can learn how to handle emergencies through a basic four-hour pet first-aid class. They'll teach you how to build a first-aid kit and an emergency kit in case you need to evacuate with your dog.

—Ines de Pablo, an emergency management specialist and founder of Wag'n Enterprises from Herndon, Virginia

or her office staff will be able to meet your specific needs.

First, consider the types of services you'll require. Do you need a facility that offers boarding and grooming? Do you expect the clinic to have state-of-the-art diagnostic equipment? Will the vet do house calls if need be? If you work during normal business hours, do you need a clinic that offers after-hours or weekend services and care?

You should also consider the clinic's proximity to your home. Is it convenient for you to visit, especially in case of emergency? Granted, sometimes the best veterinarian can be a long drive away. If that's the case, you should identify a nearby emergency clinic that you can use if something critical should occur.

The veterinarian's bedside manner is important, too, as well as whether you like and get along with the vet and the rest of the staff. When you speak with them, do you feel like they answer your questions? Do they treat you and your dog with respect? What level of doctor-patient familiarity do you want? In some clinics, you can see the same veterinarian each time you visit; in others, you may not have a choice.

Consider the clinic's various policies, such as appointment procedures, fees for visits and diagnostics, and payment policies. Does the clinic allow drop-in appointments? How much do routine wellness exams cost? Does the clinic offer discounts or payment plans?

Picking the right veterinarian and clinic can be one of the most important decisions you will make. Screen several vets in your area before choosing one. You may need to schedule an appointment to meet and interview the vet and pay a fee for the visit, but it will give you the opportunity to tour the facility, meet the office staff, and talk to the veterinarian.

When you're at the vet's office, inspect the facility for cleanliness and organization. Note the attitude of the employees. Be prepared to ask the veterinarian and the office manager questions about such things as the clinic's area of expertise, how long the clinic has been in practice, and whether the vet offers any alternative therapies. Do they speak to you in a way that you'll understand? If you're not comfortable with the doctor, the other staff members, or the facility, your dog won't be either.

FIRST VET VISIT

Your first days with your new dog should be happy ones, so it's critical that you take your Border Collie to your veterinarian within forty-eight to seventy-two hours of his arrival home. You want to make sure that you've acquired a healthy dog, whether puppy or adult, free of health problems that might not be readily noticeable.

Arrive early for your first appointment and bring the documents that came with your Border Collie. This paperwork contains important information that the doctor needs, including details about any previous vaccinations that have been given or tests that have been performed on your dog. Plan to complete some preliminary paperwork that will ask for information about

Did You Know?

Dog owners spent an average of $248 per year on routine veterinary care in 2010, according to the American Pet Product Association's 2011–2012 National Pet Owners Survey, and an average of $407 per year on surgical veterinary care.

Visiting the vet is one of the first things that you and your new Border Collie should do together.

your dog's vital statistics, activity level, previous health problems (if known), and any other pets you may have. Also plan to bring in a fresh stool sample so the vet can check for internal parasites.

A veterinary technician or assistant will escort you and your pup to an exam room and weigh your Border Collie, take his temperature, and ask questions about the reason for your visit. During the physical exam, the veterinarian will assess your dog's overall health and look for potential health problems. The vet will listen to your pup's heart and lungs; feel his abdomen, muscles, and

joints; inspect his mouth, teeth, and gums; look into his eyes, ears, and nose; and feel his coat. The doctor will keep an eye out for anything out of the ordinary and check for any congenital or other hereditary problems that have gone unnoticed. The doctor will also ask about your Border Collie's behavior, including his eating and playing habits.

Ask the doctor any questions that you may have about the breed and its known health issues, which we discuss in chapter 7. Talk to your vet about how to nurture your Border Collie's vitality through proper diet and exercise. Ask when you should have your dog spayed or neutered, and when your dog is due for vaccinations again. Request trainer and groomer recommendations from your vet. This is the time to establish a good rapport with your veterinarian so that you're comfortable with each other throughout the dog's lifetime.

UNDERSTANDING VACCINES

Dogs face a range of communicable diseases today, but these diseases can be prevented with vaccinations. A vaccine is essentially weakened or dead forms of a disease that are injected into your pet to stimulate his immune system, causing him to produce antibodies against that disease. When he's exposed to the real disease, his body recognizes the invader and his defenses fight it off.

When your Border Collie is a puppy, he gets antibodies from his mother's milk, but starting at the age of six weeks and continuing every three to four weeks until your pup reaches the age of sixteen weeks old, your puppy will receive a series of vaccinations to protect him from a range of diseases.

Seven of the most common diseases for which vaccinations are given are listed here. Whether your veterinarian inoculates against all of them depends on where you live and what viruses are prevalent. If you travel or are planning to travel with your dog, be sure to let your veterinarian know so that he or she can decide if additional vaccinations are necessary.

Rabies: Carried in the saliva of infected wildlife and transmitted through bites or abrasions, rabies attacks the nerve tissue and cause paralysis and death. It is always fatal. In most areas, proof of rabies vaccination is required when you apply for a dog's license.

Distemper: Distemper is a contagious viral disease that causes symptoms resembling a bad cold with a fever. It can include runny nose and eyes, and an upset stomach that could lead to vomiting and diarrhea. Many infected animals exhibit neurological symptoms. An incurable and deadly disease, distemper is passed through exposure to the saliva, urine, and feces of raccoons, foxes, wolves, minks, and other dogs. Young pups and senior dogs are most vulnerable to distemper.

Parvovirus: Another deadly virus, parvo attacks the inner lining of a dog's intestines. It causes bloody diarrhea that has a distinctive smell. Symptoms also include depression, loss of appetite, vomiting and collapse. As this virus replicates very quickly, prompt medical attention is needed should your Border Collie exhibit any of these signs. The vaccination is usually effective.

Hepatitis: Spread through contact with other dogs' saliva, mucus, urine, or feces, hepatitis affects the liver and kidneys. It causes depression, vomiting, abdominal pain, fever, and jaundice. The mortality rate is high, but vaccination is an effective preventive.

Leptospirosis: A highly contagious bacterium that is passed through the urine of infected dogs, rats, and wildlife, leptospirosis attacks the animal's kidneys, causing kidney failure. Symptoms include fever, appetite loss, possible diarrhea, and jaundice. Vaccinations usually prevent the disease, though the bacteria do appear in different forms and the vaccine may not protect against all of them.

Coronavirus: Rarely fatal for adult dogs but deadly to puppies, coronavirus causes a loose, watery stool and vomiting. Dehydration from the diarrhea and vomiting endangers infected puppies. The virus is spread through the stool.

Kennel cough: Tracheobronchitis (commonly known as kennel cough) is rarely deadly, but it does cause significant coughing, sneezing, and hacking, sometimes with nasal discharge and fever. Two of the most common causes of kennel cough are the parainfluenza virus and the *Bordetella bronchiseptica* bacterium. Severe cases may progress to pneumonia. Symptoms can last from several days to several weeks. As kennel cough is very contagious, dogs that frequent doggy day care, boarding kennels, training classes, groomers, dog parks, or other public places where dogs congregate should be vaccinated routinely.

Your clinic will schedule your pup's vaccinations, but typically, at the age of six to eight weeks, your breeder will have the litter vaccinated for the most common diseases—distemper, hepatitis, leptospirosis, parvovirus, and parainfluenza—with one combined injection called DHLPP. Your Border Collie will get another DHLPP shot between ten and twelve weeks and a third between fourteen and sixteen weeks.

Your pup will get his first rabies vaccine at the age of twelve weeks or older, depending on your local regulations, and his second vaccine one year later. Depending on the laws in your state, booster vaccinations may be given either annually or every three years thereafter. Dogs usually receive coronavirus and Lyme disease vaccinations only if there is a problem in the areas where they live.

Vaccines are injected either into a muscle (intramuscular) or under the skin (subcutaneous). Some vaccines for kennel cough are sprayed up the nose (intranasal). Most times, the pup won't bat an eye.

After your pup has completed his vaccinations, you'll need to return to the vet for booster shots. Some research suggests that yearly booster shots may actually be over-vaccinating our dogs, so booster protocols are changing. Some veterinarians still give annual boosters, while others give boosters every eighteen months or even every three years. Talk to your veterinarian about his suggested booster schedule.

If you adopt an adult dog who has not been vaccinated or who has an unknown vaccination history, your veterinarian will administer a rabies shot right away and will start your Border Collie on the DHLPP series with the shots spaced out the same way as for a puppy.

FIRST AID KNOW-HOW

Whether your Border Collie is a puppy or an adult, he will undoubtedly get himself into trouble at one time or another. When that day (or days!) occurs, and your dog comes inside with a gashed leg or a porcupine quill-covered snout, knowing how to properly use the tools in your first-aid kit will help you assist your dog.

Prepackaged first-aid kits can be found at your pet-specialty store, or you can gather the necessary items yourself and keep them in a prominently labeled, watertight container in an accessible spot. If you hit the road often with your dog, keep a travel-size version of your first-aid kit in your vehicle. Everyone in your family should know where the first-aid kits are kept, what they contain, and how to use each item. Your first-aid kit should include:

- Tweezers
- Scissors
- Nail clippers for dogs
- Rectal thermometer
- Tape
- Bandages (butterfly and standard)
- Elastic bandages
- Rolls of gauze
- Gauze pads of varying sizes
- Eye pads
- Cotton balls or cotton swabs
- Instant cold compress
- Antiseptic cleansing wipes
- Alcohol pads
- Saline eye wash
- Hydrogen peroxide, 3 percent (to disinfect wounds)
- Styptic powder (to stop bleeding)
- Benadryl (to stop an allergic reaction)
- Syrup of ipecac (to induce vomiting)
- Kaopectate (to treat diarrhea)
- Iodine (to sterilize wounds)
- Antibiotic ointment
- Bottle of water
- Pen and paper
- Old blanket or sheet
- Extra leash and collar
- Pen light
- Instructional pet first-aid book

Include your vet's and the local emergency pet clinic's phone numbers, too. Check your kit often and replace supplies that have been

No matter how careful you are with your precious Border Collie, sometimes unexpected injuries happen. Be prepared for an emergency by creating a canine first-aid kit. Find out what essentials you need on **DogChannel.com/Club-Border**—just click on "Downloads."

JOIN OUR ONLINE **Club Border™**

used or medications that have expired. If you don't know how to use these items, enroll in a basic first-aid course. The American Red Cross (www.redcross.org) and Pet Tech (www.pettech.net) both offer nationwide courses for dog owners that will teach you how to do things like handle a dog who is in shock, who has a fracture, or who requires CPR. If a course isn't available in your area, ask your veterinarian for advice.

EVERYDAY PROBLEMS

Acting quickly in case of an injury or emergency can help your Border Collie and could even save his life. If your dog is hurt, first assess whether he needs immediate veterinary care. Major traumas, such as animal bites and fractures, should be handled by a professional; minor injuries and illnesses, such as cuts, scrapes, and mild stomach upset, can be managed at home. First, you should know your dog's normal vitals:

Pulse: Typical pulse rate is 60 to 140 beats per minute in an active, alert dog. It should be strong and robust. You can feel your dog's pulse by palpating the lower chest wall behind his shoulder or by feeling the pulse in his femoral artery, which is located high on the inside of each thigh.

Temperature: Normal canine temperature is 100 to 102 degrees Fahrenheit. Check your dog's temperature by using a small thermometer; lubricate it well with petroleum jelly and insert into the rectum for about one minute.

Mucous membrane color: The color of a dog's gums should be pink (when resting) or red (when active), thanks to the blood vessels in the mouth. A dog who is in shock, anemic, overheating, or losing blood may show pale or white gums; a dog with respiratory problems may show gray or blue gums.

Breathing rate: This is about twelve to twenty breaths per minute. Your dog's breathing rate indicates how well his respiratory system is functioning. Pain, fever, fear, or excitement may cause an increase in his breathing rate.

If your dog is outside of these general ranges, he may be dealing with an injury or trauma. Examine your dog for cuts, broken bones, or insect bites. Watch his reactions as you run your hands gently over his body, and make note of any irregularities.

Rush to the Vet

Whether out in the field working or in the backyard playing, a Border Collie could find himself in a medical emergency at any time. A dog who is bleeding, going into shock, experiencing respiratory failure, or overheating needs you to stabilize him and get him to the veterinarian or emergency clinic. If your

Did You Know? Pet health insurance may seem like just an extra expense, but it could save you thousands of dollars should your Border Collie require emergency surgery or veterinary care. Like human health-care plans, pet plans vary by provider, but most will cover annual exams, vaccinations, flea control, heartworm protection, hospitalizations, accidents, radiology, surgeries, and even cancer therapy. After you meet your deductible, the insurance company will reimburse you for covered costs. Before choosing one, look at different plans and weigh your options.

dog is exhibiting any of these symptoms, get him professional help immediately:

- Shock
- Respiratory failure
- Drowning
- Electric shock
- Airway obstruction
- Profuse bleeding
- Cardiac arrest
- Anaphylaxis (from insect or snake bite)
- Poison ingestion

Seek professional help in these and other life-threatening situations, such as severe injury or trauma. If you must rush your dog to the clinic, always call ahead to describe the nature of the problem and let the staff know that you're on your way.

In-Home Care

Bumps, bruises, scrapes, insect stings, and minor injuries and ailments can be handled at home. Monitor your dog if he's experiencing mild vomiting and diarrhea to make sure that his condition is not worsening. Keep an eye on your pup if he's bleeding or scratching a sting. An injured pup doesn't have to result in an expensive visit to the vet—as long as you know what to do.

Bleeding: Bleeding can occur from just about any injury; how you treat it depends on the wound and its severity. If your pup is bruised, apply an ice pack to the area for fifteen-minute intervals until the swelling subsides. For minor cuts and scrapes, wipe the wound clean with an alcohol pad and apply pressure with a clean gauze pad until the bleeding stops; cover the wound with a bandage. Severe wounds will require a vet check, so apply direct pressure or a tourniquet, if necessary, and get to a clinic as soon as possible.

Heat exhaustion or heat stroke: Common among active dogs in warm climates, dehydration, heat exhaustion, or the more dangerous heat stroke can occur when dogs are overexercised in hot weather. It can also occur when dogs are left in cars on warm days or when kennel areas aren't ventilated properly. Symptoms of heat exhaustion include rapid breathing, panting, and drooling. The risk of heat stroke increases as the dog's body temperature rises (104 degrees Fahrenheit or higher). A severely overheated dog could go into shock and will likely die without proper veterinary treatment. If you notice signs of heat exhaustion or worse, immediately get your Border Collie out of the heat. Spray him with cool water and apply cool cloths to his body. Do not use ice or cold water, as this will constrict the blood vessels and interfere with the cooling process. Call your veterinarian or emergency clinic immediately. Heat stroke is an emergency situation, and your vet will instruct you to bring the dog in once his body temperature has stabilized.

Vomiting and diarrhea: An indicator of problems with your dog's digestive system, vomiting or diarrhea can be caused by anything from spicy food to ingestion of a toxic substance. If the condition doesn't seem severe, feed your dog a bland diet of plain, cooked chicken and rice for the first twelve hours and monitor his symptoms. If his condition doesn't improve, contact your veterinarian. Excessive vomiting or diarrhea can cause dehydration, so make sure your pup drinks plenty of water.

Insect stings: If you suspect that a bee, wasp, or other stinging insect has stung your Border Collie, first determine the site of the sting and remove the stinger by carefully scraping it out or removing it with tweezers; you may need to shave the area to remove the stinger and treat the area. Wash the area thoroughly, bathe it with alcohol, and watch for swelling. Some dogs are allergic to bee stings and may present the following symptoms:

• Swelling at the sting site or on the face
• Hives
• Redness or extreme whiteness
• Fever

• Muscle aches, joint pain, and lameness
• Vomiting and/or diarrhea
• Difficultly breathing

If your dog exhibits any of these symptoms, call your vet right away. He may recommend an antihistamine to combat some of the allergic reaction. As with any injury, monitor the dog and, if symptoms worsen, schedule an appointment with your veterinarian. It's better to be safe than sorry.

Keep your Border Collie active, alert, and fit with regular veterinary visits and preventive care.

I n addition to taking your Border Collie to the veterinarian for his regular checkups, you'll want to do everything you can to maintain his health and wellness between visits by feeding him a top-notch diet and giving him plenty of exercise—but that's not all. You'll also want to be aware of the diseases that can affect the breed so that you can prevent any problems—or at least catch them early.

In this chapter, you'll learn how to handle the different health challenges, both internal and external, that Border Collies can face. From genetic and congenital defects to environmental villains such as parasites, these conditions and critters can be identified and managed by the smart dog owner.

BORDER COLLIE PARTICULARS

Living to an average age of twelve—with some as old as seventeen—Border Collies are sound dogs, but there are certain

Did You Know?

A dog with a cough or cold should be treated the same as his human counter-part: give him plenty of warmth and rest. If his cold does not respond quickly to such treatment or if he appears weak and shows other symptoms, call your veterinarian. Your dog could be suffering from a more serious ailment, such as distemper, hepatitis, or heartworm infestation.

physical defects and physiological conditions that can be seen in the breed and of which you should be aware. Your breeder should be forthcoming about discussing these problems with you.

Keep an eye on your pup, and if you see any abnormalities, let your veterinarian know right away. Any dog found to have a hereditary disorder should be spayed or neutered; responsible breeders and owners do not want to pass on ailments to future generations.

Collie Eye Anomaly

Present from birth, collie eye anomaly (CEA) is a congenital, recessively inherited eye defect that affects a range of collie breeds, including the Border Collie. The disorder, which is not a progressive disease, prevents the dog's eye from developing normally. The disease's effects range from minor vision problems to total blindness. It can appear in one or both eyes.

The incidence of CEA in Border Collies in North America is about 2.5 percent, according to the American Border Collie Association (ABCA); the carrier rate is close to 25 percent. Before the pup's three-month birthday, have a board-certified veterinary ophthalmologist examine your dog to determine whether he is affected. Because of the age guidelines, breeders should conduct this test on their litters.

A dog with CEA can live a happy and productive life if his owners keep his living area as consistent as possible. His food and water bowls, crate, bed, and toys should always remain in the same places. Border Collies with moderate to severe vision problems will not likely be working dogs, but they will make excellent farm and house companions if given the right environment.

DNA testing by companies such as OptiGen, Inc. (www.optigen.com) can determine if a puppy carries the CEA gene.

Hip Dysplasia

Hip dysplasia (HD) is one of the most prevalent diseases in the Border Collie. Rapid growth, exercise, nutrition, and heredity play roles in the occurrence of the disease, which impacts the ball-and-socket hip joint. The round head of the femur, or thigh bone, should fit perfectly into the acetabulum (socket of the pelvic bone). An x-ray of a good hip shows the socket as being perfectly round, while an x-ray of a dysplastic hip shows the socket as shallow or flattened, which causes the round end of the femur to slip and rub on the bone, causing pressure and pain. A dysplastic dog will eventually develop arthritis in the joint.

Some affected dogs are lucky enough to show no signs or symptoms, but being a highly active working dog, a Border Collie with HD will often show some degree of lameness or limping. He may also have trouble getting up, may move with a side-to-side swaying gait, or may "bunny hop"—move their back feet in unison—when walking or running. Signs of severe dysplasia may be present as early as eight months of age.

Treatment for hip dysplasia can be medical or surgical. Veterinarians will recommend weight reduction, restricted exercise, controlled physical therapy to maintain and strengthen muscle tone, anti-inflammatory drugs, joint-fluid modifiers, and dietary supplements. Surgical treatment involves procedures that restore joint and limb functions, reduce pain and arthritis, and prevent joint dislocation.

When you speak with breeders before you acquire your puppy, ask them whether

Good breeders look for healthy eyes in their breeding stock to reduce the incidence of hereditary eye disease in future generations.

Puppies are vulnerable to not only worms but also to many things that can kill them with almost no warning. I learned that a sluggish pup is often a tiny step away from being a dead pup. They don't have the resistance of older dogs. As well as receiving proper prevention, puppies must be watched closely for any signs of illness.

—Bruce Fogt, Border Collie owner and trainer in Sidney, Ohio

they screen their breeding stock for dysplasia, which can be detected by x-ray. The Orthopedic Foundation of Animals (OFA) is an organization that provides a screening service for all breeds to determines whether dogs are dysplastic or normal. The x-rays are examined, and dogs are given ratings based on hip quality. Your breeder should also be able to provide you with OFA certification for the parents of the puppy you wish to purchase.

In some cases, owners of dogs with HD can manage their pets' pain and give them long and happy lives. In other cases, the condition is so disabling that the dog's quality of life is severely compromised. You cannot tell simply by looking at a puppy whether he has healthy hips, so only buy a puppy whose parents have been tested and certified as having normal hips. Good breeders will have all potential breeding stock tested so that affected dogs are not included in their breeding programs. A simple screening procedure can help breeders reduce the incidence of the disease and can prevent owners from experiencing a great deal of heartbreak.

Flea Allergy Dermatitis

Flea allergy dermatitis (FAD) is also referred to as flea bite allergic dermatitis or flea bite hypersensitivity. One of the most common skin diseases of animals worldwide, this is not a genetic disease per se, but it occurs in dogs that are naturally hypersensitive to flea bites, including Border Collies. When the flea's histamine- and enzyme-filled saliva enters the site of the flea bite, an allergic reaction can occur.

Dogs with FAD will often itch and scratch their rear ends. Some may develop papules or areas of raised skin that range in severity on the lower back, base of the tail, thighs, and the area between the thighs. FAD can cause chronic hair loss, thickening and darkening of the skin, and sometimes bacterial skin disease caused by staphylococcal bacteria. The skin may become raw and red and have an oozing, wet appearance. Acute, moist lesions of the skin are often referred to as hot spots; if the areas become infected, the dog will need antibiotics.

If your Border Collie develops an allergic reaction to flea bites, even one flea can cause a serious problem, so an effective flea-control program will be essential. Use a veterinary-recommended flea- and tick-control preventive on your pet, and control the itchy critters inside and outside your home with diligent pest management (discussed later in this chapter).

Osteochondritis Dissecans

Osteochondritis dissecans (OCD), is a genetic disease seen in young, fast-growing, active dogs of medium and large breeds. Characterized by the degeneration of bone underlying the cartilage of joints, OCD is often accompanied by a rupture or break in the cartilage itself. The disease, which can be diagnosed by x-ray, usually becomes evident when the dog is less than a year old, during periods of rapid growth.

The painful defect, which occurs most commonly in one or both of the dog's shoulders, causes inflamed joints and limping. In mild cases, bed rest and restricted activity will reduce inflammation and pain, facilitating healing. In serious cases, the dog may need surgery to remove defective cartilage and cartilage fragments found in the joint. The success rate of surgeries performed before the development of arthritis is excellent.

Progressive Retinal Atrophy

Another inherited eye disease that can affect Border Collies is progressive retinal atrophy (PRA). PRA is the result of a gradual degeneration of the cells around the retina; it worsens and eventually results in blindness. The disease incidence in the breed is very low in North America, according to the American Border Collie Association (ABCA).

Age of onset varies, but an early symptom of PRA is reduced vision in dim lighting conditions. As the disease progresses, the dog may be reluctant to wander in the yard after dark, preferring lighted doorways, and may have a hard time marking a moving target. Eventually, the night

Generally, you can prevent parasites by limiting your dog's exposure to other animals' urine and feces, giving him a heartworm preventive as prescribed by your veterinarian, and applying a flea and tick preventive (available through your vet or at pet-supply stores) to his coat.

blindness progresses to loss of daytime vision and then to total blindness.

No cure or treatment for PRA exists, but testing is available to determine if your dog is affected. An exam by a member of the American College of Veterinary Ophthalmologists that shows that your Border Collie is clear of PRA will earn the dog certification from the Canine Eye Registration Foundation (CERF), an organization that maintains an eye-health database for genetic eye diseases in dogs. Yearly exams are needed to maintain CERF status, and they are recommended because PRA can present itself later in life.

Focal/Multifocal Acquired Retinopathy

Focal/multifocal acquired retinopathy (FMAR) is an inflammatory eye disease common in working breeds, including Border Collies. FMAR is characterized by bull's eye-patterned lesions, sometimes called distemper scars or worm scars, that accumulate in the retina, causing impaired vision or even blindness. It is usually worse in one eye than the other. The age of onset varies; males tend to acquire it more frequently than females. FMAR appears to be caused by environmental factors; the ABCA notes no heritable pattern in the disease's occurrence.

PREVENTING PARASITES

While breed-specific genetic and congenital health problems can be managed, another type of canine health problems can be prevented: parasites. You and your dog can avoid the pain, frustration, and itchiness of internal and external parasites as long as you give your pup preventive medication and know what to look for.

Not a frou-frou companion dog or couch-potato pooch, the Border Collie thrives outside, at work, doing what he does best: outthinking and herding livestock. Even if he's not driving ewes across the field or shedding a sheep into a pen, your Border Collie will be spending plenty of time outdoors, where he runs the risk of picking up all kinds of "hitchhikers," including internal and external parasites.

Parasites are tiny organisms that live off of other living organisms. These little blood and nutrient thieves come in all shapes and sizes, from single-celled protozoa and small insects (such as fleas) to long intestinal tapeworms. Both internal and external parasites latch on to the host animal and draw nourishment from the animal without providing any benefit in return. Sometimes, the parasites weaken the host (your dog) so severely that the host may die.

In most cases, if your Border Collie picks up parasites, it will be from exposure to contaminated environments. For example, your dog may romp through a grassy field and bring home some fleas or ticks, or he may ingest a strange dog's feces and develop an internal parasite. Here's what you need to know about internal and external parasites common to canines and how you can prevent your Border Collie from bringing home these troublesome tagalongs.

Internal Parasites: The Skinny on Worms

Internal parasites are a part of pet ownership. They aren't pleasant, but you need to address them to keep your pet healthy. Because these pests live inside your Border Collie, you can't see the damage they're causing. It can take quite some time before your dog exhibits external signs of being affected by an internal parasite problem.

Your veterinarian can detect most internal parasites through testing and microscopic examination of a stool sample, which often contains the eggs, remains, or even larvae of the parasite in an affected dog. Your vet will prescribe a treatment, and after it runs its course, you will need to bring in another stool sample to be sure that the treatment was successful.

Various types of internal parasites affect dogs; some are more dangerous than others. The following are the most common.

Hookworms: Hookworms, which can cause fatal anemia in puppies, attach themselves to the small intestine and suck the dog's blood. After the worms detach and move to a new location, the wound continues to bleed, causing bloody diarrhea, which owners often notice as the first sign of hookworm infestation. Like other internal parasites, hookworm eggs are passed through the stool and can live in the soil, so good sanitation will prevent the worms' spread. Canine hookworms can affect humans, usually causing an itchy rash.

Hookworm treatment involves giving the dog an oral deworming tablet or liquid, followed by another dose one month later. The first treatment destroys the adult worms living in the dog, and the second treatment destroys the next generation. After the second treatment, your vet will do another fecal exam to ensure that the parasites are gone.

Roundworms: Roundworms, which are long, white worms that live in the dog's intestines, are fairly common in puppies, as they are often transmitted in utero to the puppies from their mother. They can be seen in feces and vomit, and the eggs are transmitted through the stool. A dog infested with roundworms is thin and may have a dull coat and a pot belly. A stool analysis will confirm diagnosis.

Roundworms are zoonotic, meaning that they can affect humans, too. Roundworm infection can cause neurological damage and blindness in humans. Small children are at high risk for becoming infected through the environment as they play and may accidentally ingest eggs or larvae. Good sanitation will prevent the spread of roundworms to other dogs and to humans.

As with treatment for hookworm infestation, treatment for roundworms involves an oral deworming medication that is repeated several times to ensure that subsequent generations of the parasite are destroyed.

Whipworms: These internal parasites live in the dog's large intestine, where

Did You Know?

Ringworm isn't a parasite at all. It's a contagious fungus that infects the skin and causes a red, ring-shaped, itchy rash. It spreads through contact with other animals. Ringworm responds well to treatment, but because it's so contagious to people and other animals, you must follow an eradication plan diligently.

A dog that spends a lot of time outdoors, such as the Border Collie, may be at a greater risk of exposure to parasites, but there are ways to protect your dog.

they feed on blood. A heavy infestation of whipworms can be fatal to adults and puppies because it can cause severe diarrhea. Dogs infested with whipworms look lethargic and thin. Whipworm eggs are passed in the feces and can live in the soil for years, so dogs that dig in the dirt or eat grass can pick up eggs.

If caught early, whipworm can be treated with deworming medications that must be administered over an extended period of time. Because of the long maturation cycle of young worms, a second deworming is needed seventy-five days after the first one. Additional doses may also be necessary.

Heartworms: Dangerous yet preventable parasites, heartworms live in an infected dog's upper heart and arteries, damaging the blood vessel walls and causing poor circulation, which ultimately causes heart failure. The parasite is spread by mosquitoes. Adult heartworms produce tiny worms, which circulate throughout the infected dog's bloodstream. When a mosquito bites the dog, the mosquito picks up the worms and transmits them when it bites another dog.

The first signs of heartworm infestation include breathing difficulty, coughing, and lack of energy, though some dogs show no signs until it's too late. To confirm a diagnosis, your vet will take a blood test to look for worms; he may also do an x-ray. If the test results are positive, your vet will give your dog medication to kill the worms.

Preventive medications, however, are the best remedy and are much safer than treating your dog after he's infected. Preventives are easily available from your veterinarian, and they're very effective. If heartworm is prevalent in your area and your dog is more than six months old, your veterinarian will first do a blood test to determine whether your dog is infected. Puppies younger than six months old can be started on heartworm prevention without testing. If your Border Collie receives a clean bill of health, your veterinarian will prescribe a safe heartworm preventive for him, which is usually given orally once a month. Many of these preventive medications also provide protection against roundworms, hookworms, and whipworms.

Giardia: Commonly passed through wild animals, Giardia, an intestinal parasitic protozoan, affects humans and animals and causes diarrhea and lethargy. It is often found in mountain streams, but it can also be found in puddles or stagnant water. Your veterinarian will test for giardiasis and can prescribe treatment in the form of an oral antibiotic.

Tapeworms: Dogs most commonly acquire tapeworms when they eat infected fleas that are carrying tapeworm eggs. Rabbits carry another less common type of tapeworm, and dogs can become infected if they eat infected rabbits or rabbit entrails. Tapeworms live in an animal's intestine, where they attach to the intestinal wall and absorb nutrients. They grow by creating new segments, which can often be seen around the dog's rectum or in his stool as small, rice-like pieces. Your veterinarian can treat tapeworms with an

By giving your dog medication to prevent heartworm infestation, you're also protecting him from other worms, such as hookworms and roundworms.

it's a **Fact**

oral dewormer or a series of injections, but a good flea-control program is the best prevention against tapeworm infestation.

External Parasites: Fleas and Ticks and Mites, Oh My!

Fleas and ticks (and other bothersome bugs) are not fun on your dog—or in your house! These parasites live off your pet's blood. They spread disease and can transmit internal parasites, as you read in the previous section. Thankfully, these pests can be controlled, so you and your Border Collie can enjoy the great outdoors together.

Fleas: Fleas are small, crescent-shaped insects that suck the blood from their canine hosts. With their six legs and huge abdomens, they can jump surprisingly far in proportion to their size. Their bites cause allergic reactions in dogs and their humans,

causing itching, discomfort, and misery. Border Collies are among the breeds that are particularly sensitive to flea bites.

Fleas are small, but they're not invisible. If you see just one flea crawling on your Border Collie or hopping in your carpet, for example, chances are very high that there are many more, both on your dog and in your home. You may see your pup scratching and biting to rid himself of the parasites, or you may see him rolling on the floor to ease the itchiness. When combing through your dog's coat, you may see white flea eggs or flea "dirt" (feces), which can resemble specks of black pepper.

In large numbers—especially on a sensitive-skinned dog like your Border Collie—fleas can cause anemia and severe allergic reactions that can lead to open sores and possibly a secondary infection. Fleas also spread internal parasites, such as tape-

To remove a tick from your Border Collie's skin, have him lie down and hold still. Using tweezers to grab hold of the tick as close as possible to the dog's skin, pull the tick straight out, gently but firmly. Drop the bloodsucker in a glass filled with water or alcohol (which you'll flush down the toilet later) and apply a little antibiotic ointment to your pup's wound.

worms. In the past, fleas carried bubonic plague. These parasites are more than a nuisance—they're a real threat. You'll have to treat your dog, your home, and your yard to prevent fleas from returning. It's fortunate for dogs and their owners that more flea-control options exist now than ever before:

• Topical treatments: These are liquids that are applied to the dog's skin between the shoulder blades. The product is absorbed through the dog's skin into his system, and the fleas are killed when they bite the animal or when their reproduction cycle is altered. Different topical flea-control formulas have different active ingredients and different methods of application. Ask your veterinarian which product is right for your Border Collie and how the product should be applied. These products are

Always picking up after your pup gives your Border Collie a clean place to play and relax.

usually administered once a month as a preventive measure.

- Systemic treatments: These treatments are administered orally. When the flea bites the dog, the chemical in the medication is transmitted to the flea, which (depending on the product) either prevents the flea's eggs from developing or kills the adult fleas so that the population dies off.

- Insect growth regulators (IGRs): IGRs stop immature fleas from maturing and prevent them from reproducing, so the population eventually ceases to exist. Dispensed as foggers, as sprays, and in disc form, IGRs can be used in the environment to stop bug populations from thriving. You'll need to treat your house and the shady areas of your yard for complete flea eradication.

If you prefer natural external-parasite control, several plant-based products are available over the counter. Some of the more popular ones include pyrethrins, which are derived from chrysanthemums, and citrus-based derivatives. They both work to knock down the flea population, but they do little to eradicate an infestation.

Ticks: Ticks are eight-legged bloodsuckers that latch on to their hosts, embed their heads into the skin, and suck until they become engorged with blood. They won't overrun your home like fleas can, but they will cause misery as they suck your pup's blood. Sometimes the area around a tick bite can become red and painful. Ticks prefer the areas around your dog's head, neck, ears, and feet, and the warm areas between the legs and the body.

Ticks carry blood-transmitted diseases, including Lyme disease and Rocky Mountain spotted fever. Lyme disease is carried by deer ticks, which are small (about the size of a sesame seed) and can be hard to spot. It is characterized by a lingering fever, joint pain, and neurological problems. Rocky Mountain spotted fever is characterized by muscle pain, high fever, and skin sores.

Some flea-control products also deter ticks, but the best thing to do is check your Border Collie after he has spent time in potentially tick-infested areas, such as woods, brush, and tall grasses. During the spring and summer, inspect your dog daily, paying close attention to the aforementioned areas in which ticks like to burrow.

Mange mites: Mange, caused by microscopic mites, results in swelling of the dog's skin and itchy, pus-filled scabs. The disease comes in two varieties: sarcoptic mange, which is contagious to people and other pets; and demodectic mange, which is not contagious. Your veterinarian will need to do a skin scraping to determine which variety is plaguing your dog.

If your pup is scratching but you've found no signs of fleas, he may have mange. Mange mites like the areas around the elbows, hocks, ears, and face. They will need to be identified by your veterinarian, who will inspect your pup's skin scraping under a microscope.

Dogs suffering from mange may scratch themselves fiercely. Patches of skin look red and scaly, and an affected dog may have areas of thinning hair around the eyes, around the mouth, and on the fronts of the legs. In more advanced infestations, oozing sores may lead to secondary infections. Treatment involves bathing with medicated shampoos, possibly antibiotics or steroids to relieve the itching symptoms, and possibly injections or an oral medication.

Your Border Collie's diet gives him the fuel he needs to get through the day. Your high-energy herding dog with his hearty appetite requires a healthy diet that provides the right amount of protein, carbohydrates, fat, vitamins, and minerals per serving, especially after a long day's work moving ewes or practicing agility maneuvers.

With so many food options available, how do you choose which diet is best? Should you go with a commercial formula? What about making your dog's food from scratch? How do you ensure balanced nutrition? To make the right choice, it's important to first understand the essential elements in a carnivore's diet.

FUELING A CARNIVORE

Before they became the domesticated pets that we know today, dogs scavenged and preyed on small animals. They also foraged for food, eating berries, grains, and other plant matter when necessary. This diet gave them the protein, fat, carbohydrates, vitamins, and minerals they needed for a complete and healthy diet.

Active working breeds like the Border Collie should not be fed too close to periods of strenuous activity or exercise to reduce the risk of a serious condition called bloat, or gastric torsion (twisting of the stomach).

it's a Fact

As a ranch hand or house pet, your Border Collie requires the same basic nutrients as his forebears did, but each dog has different individual requirements. Young pups need a diet formulated for growth, so puppy diets contain a larger percentage of nutrients such as protein and carbohydrates to support healthy—but not rapid—growth. Adults need a diet formulated for maintenance. They require enough calories and nutrients to support their normal activities and bodily functions, but not so many that they gain weight. As they age, senior dogs need to take in fewer calories to prevent obesity as their metabolism changes.

Let's take a closer look at the role of the various nutrients and how they keep your Border Collie healthy and happy.

Protein Power

Your Border Collie's body uses protein for growing, developing hair and skin, producing hormones, building muscle mass, regulating the metabolism, and repairing damaged tissue.

In many premium brands of dog food, the protein source is the first ingredient listed. Beef, chicken, turkey, lamb, and duck are among the proteins most commonly used. Other protein sources include fish, fish meal, liver, eggs, milk, and milk products. A growing number of food makers are even using alternative proteins, such as kangaroo, buffalo, bison, and goat, in their diets.

Some grains and beans (such as rice, wheat, corn, barley, and soy) also contain protein. They're not complete sources of protein like animal-based proteins are, but when combined with other food ingredients, they can provide many of the amino acids that dogs require.

Border Collie puppies thrive on foods that contain about 28 percent protein; adult Border Collies typically maintain themselves on foods that contain 22 percent protein. When you choose a diet for your Border Collie, don't pick one based on the formula's protein percentage alone; the protein source matters, too. In general, the lower-priced foods use lesser-grade protein sources that are harder for your dog to digest.

Crazy for Carbs

Carbohydrates, which are sugars and starches found in plant foods, provide the quick energy that Border Collies need to drive livestock, exercise, and play. Making up about 50 percent of your dog's diet, carbohydrates also provide fiber, which is essential for proper bowel function. Common sources of fiber are rice, grains, peas, pasta, and even potatoes.

Carbohydrates can also be fillers in dog foods. Corn and rice are often used to bulk up lower-priced foods, while premium dog foods contain high-quality complex carbohydrates to give the dog fiber and sustained energy.

Too many cereal grains can result in a hyped-up Border Collie. If your dog is bouncing off the walls, take a look at the types and amounts of carbohydrates in his diet. He may need a food with fewer or higher-quality carbs. Fillers also cause your dog to eliminate more often, which means more trips to the bathroom.

Healthy Fats, Healthy Coat

Fats and oils do more than make foods taste good; they provide energy and help your Border Collie feel satisfied. Fats are needed to break down certain vitamins, such as vitamins A, D, K, and E. Unsaturated fatty

Good nutrition keeps your Border Collie fueled up for his active lifestyle.

Believe it or not, during your Border Collie's lifetime, you'll buy a few hundred pounds of dog food! Go to **DogChannel.com/Club-Border** and download a chart that outlines the cost of dog food.

acids, such as oleic and linoleic acids, also support skin and coat health, making your Border Collie's coat shimmer and shine.

Dog foods typically contain anywhere from 8 to 18 percent fat, depending on the manufacturer and formula. If your Border Collie's coat is looking dull, consider a food that has a higher percentage of unsaturated fats. If he's looking a little overweight, switch to a lower-fat diet after talking with your veterinarian.

Vitamins and Minerals

In addition to proteins, carbohydrates, and fats, dogs require vitamins, which help the body fight disease, absorb minerals, regulate metabolism, and grow and function normally. Plant and animal foods naturally contain vitamins.

The body maintains and stores fat-soluble vitamins in the body's liver and fatty tissues, and water-soluble vitamins, such as vitamins B and C, are flushed out daily and must be replaced. The right balance of vitamins is crucial to your Border Collie's health and well-being.

Minerals, such as calcium, iron, phosphorous, and nitrates, are elements and inorganic compounds that the body needs for proper growth and function. Minerals help maintain the salt levels in the bloodstream and build bones and teeth. Dogs require a balance of major minerals and trace minerals, including copper and potassium.

Most commercial and premium diets already contain all of the vitamins and minerals that your dog needs in the proper proportions. Your veterinarian may recommend some supplements for specific needs, such as glucosamine for a senior dog suffering from arthritis or multivitamins for a dog that's eating a homemade diet. Always follow your veterinarian's advice and consult him before adding any supplements to your Border Collie's diet.

REFRESH WITH WATER

Protein, carbs, fats, vitamins, and minerals are important components in your Border Collie's food, but he needs to drink, too. Like our own bodies, our dogs' bodies require plenty of water to function normally. Water keeps the digestive system working, the mucus membranes lubricated, and the cells replicating. It flushes their systems and keeps their bodies free from harmful toxins. Dogs, like humans, need water to live.

With normal play and exercise, your pup will need to replenish his body with water frequently. On hot days or after long days working the herd or training for agility, your dog will need even more water. Always have plenty of fresh, cold water available for your Border Collie.

NOTABLE & QUOTABLE

Commercial food is easy: you open the bag and pour it out, and you don't have to worry about the nutritional facets of the food. It's ready to feed. If you're going to make your own food, you play the role of quality-control person, nutritionist, and food preparer, so there's additional work associated with it.

—Sean Delaney, DVM, Dipl. ACVN, *a veterinary nutritionist and nutrition professor based in Davis, California*

Your Border Collie's metabolism changes as he ages, so you will need to adjust his diet accordingly.

Not all water is good, though. Stagnant water in an outdoor bucket or pond may harbor bacteria that could make your pet sick. Water from the toilet may contain chemicals that could harm your dog. If possible, do not let your Border Collie drink from vessels other than his water bowls. It's better to be safe than sorry!

TYPES OF DOG FOOD

Once you understand the importance of the ingredients in your Border Collie's food, you can evaluate the different options available at your pet-supply store. The most common forms of dog food are dry food, semi-moist food, and canned food. More stores are also offering alternative diet options, including

JOIN OUR ONLINE Club Border™

Feeding your Border Collie is part of your daily routine. Have some fun online playing "Feed the Border Collie," an exclusive game found only on **DogChannel.com/Club-Border—** just click on "Games."

frozen foods and dehydrated mixes.

No matter what type of food you choose, each morsel should be chock full of nutrients. Because your Border Collie is such an energetic dog with a high metabolism, every bite of food should contain what he needs to keep him going.

Dry Food

It may not look too appetizing to humans, but kibble (dry food) is enjoyed by many dogs. The kibble's shape, size, texture, smell, and taste have been researched and tested by scientists and veterinary nutritionists who develop recipes, conduct feeding trials, and check for complete nutrition to ensure each kibble meets the standards of the US Food and Drug Administration (FDA).

Dry food is often the least expensive type of food on the shelf. It's made by cooking the ingredients together in big batches, forming it into kibble-size bites, and baking it. Dogs can digest dry food easily, and the kibble's crunch helps keep your dog's teeth tartar free.

You can add variety to your Border Collie's dry food diet by feeding canned food periodically or offering a mix of wet and dry food at mealtimes. You can also add water to the kibble to soften it, or occasionally put some healthy (and safe) table scraps in his dinner bowl to keep his meals interesting.

For Border Collies who have dental problems, are recovering from surgery, or are just finicky, dry food poses a challenge. A dog with dental problems can't chew the hard pieces of food, and the dried morsels may not be appealing enough for a Border Collie who isn't feeling well or has very discriminating taste buds. Dogs who are ill may need to eat semi-moist or canned food until they recover, and you might have to experiment with different flavors or different combinations of dry and wet food until you find something to please a picky pooch.

Semi-moist Varieties

Semi-moist foods are soft to the bite and come in different shapes and sizes, from kibble-size morsels to patties to chunks that resemble pieces of meat and vegetables. They often come in resealable pouches to keep the moisture locked in.

Like dry foods, semi-moist foods are formulated to serve the nutritional needs of the dog. The benefit of semi-moist foods compared to kibble is the water content, which makes it easier to chew for elderly dogs or those with dental problems. The food also smells more appetizing to finicky dogs, and the softer texture may be more palatable to some.

A semi-moist's food look, taste, and texture, however, is often achieved through the addition of chemicals, sugars, and colors. Be sure to read the label and check the food's nutritional content before feeding. Be on the lookout for a high amount of corn syrup, sugar, or other sweeteners that provide empty calories. Also beware that the softer texture can cause tartar

Did You Know?

To keep your Border Collie's dry food fresh and bug-free, store it in an airtight container in a cool, dry place. If you pour it into a bin, don't discard the bag completely. Save the label for future reference and jot down the lot number located on the bag of food in case you need it.

Want to play doggy chef? Try making one of these mouthwatering treats for your Border Collie. Remember that treats should be enjoyed in moderation, along with your dog's regular well-balanced meals.

Doggy Egg Rolls

2 cups whole-wheat flour
¼ cup vegetable oil
Water, as needed
1 boneless, skinless chicken breast,
   steamed or broiled
1 small bunch spinach
2 Tbsp grated carrots

Preheat oven to 375 degrees Fahrenheit. Mince the chicken breast and set aside. Cut the flour and oil together using knives or a pastry cutter until the mixture resembles coarse meal. Add water by the teaspoonful until the mixture holds together and can be formed into a ball. Roll out the dough to a ⅛-inch thickness and cut into 4-inch rectangles. Place a teaspoon of minced chicken in a row along one edge of one of the rectangles. Add some spinach and carrots, dab the edges of the dough with water, fold in the sides, and roll into an egg roll shape. Seal the edge with water. Repeat with each dough rectangle. Arrange egg rolls on a greased or lined cookie sheet and bake for 20 minutes or until light golden.

Day-After-Thanksgiving Turkey Treats

½ cup dark-meat turkey, cooked and shredded
1 cup water
1¾ cups whole-wheat flour
2 cups diced sweet potatoes, cooked until tender
2 large eggs

Preheat oven to 350 degrees Fahrenheit. Combine all of the ingredients and mix until sticky. Drop the dough in rounded teaspoons onto a greased or lined cookie sheet. Bake for about 20 minutes or until golden brown. Store treats in an airtight container in the refrigerator.

to build up on a dog's teeth, resulting in dental problems.

Canned Food

Foods that look like ground meat or chunks in hearty gravy look good not only to dogs but also to their owners, who may want to give their pets something that resembles their own food. Available in myriad flavors, combinations, and recipes, canned foods combine all of the nutrients in a way that caters to many dogs' taste buds.

A healthy coat and alert demeanor are two signs that your dog's diet is doing its job.

Canned food has a high water content—up to 70 percent water by weight—which supplies the Border Collie with much-needed wet stuff, but this also means that it takes more wet food to give a dog the calories and nutrition that he needs. Its taste attracts finicky eaters, and it is easier to bite and chew than kibble. Unopened canned food has a long shelf life and is easy to bring along for dogs traveling to shows or competitive trials.

Despite its benefits, canned food generally costs more than dry food. It can't be left out in your dog's bowl because it can spoil, and leftovers must be refrigerated and used within a few days. Some Border Collie owners worry about the additives and preservatives in canned food, which can cause tartar to build on the teeth and may cause diarrhea in some dogs.

READING DOG FOOD LABELS

Dog food labels contain basic information about the food in the package, including its caloric content, nutrient content, and ingredients. Pet foods are regulated by the FDA's Center for Veterinary Medicine and must contain certain information on their labels, including:

- **Feeding instructions:** Guidelines for how much to feed your dog based on his weight.
- **Guaranteed analysis:** Nutrients in the food, by percentage. It lists minimum levels of crude protein and crude fat, maximum levels of crude fiber and moisture, and measurements of additives, vitamins, and minerals.
- **Ingredients:** The formula's contents listed in descending order by amount. Often, a form of protein is the first ingredient, followed by grains, fats,

NOTABLE & QUOTABLE

The most important thing to prolong a dog's lifespan and reduce the incidence of disease is to restrict access to food so that the dog remains in a lean body condition—not skinny, but lean. In larger dogs, which are prone to arthritis, you can prolong their lives by as much as two years.

— Richard Hill, VetMB, Ph.D., MRCVS, Dipl. ACVN, a veterinary nutritionist and nutrition professor at the University of Florida College of Veterinary Medicine in Gainesville, Florida

additives, and preservatives. If a food does not have a quality protein source as its first ingredient, look for one that does.

- **Nutritional adequacy statement:** Whether the food provides complete and balanced nutrition for a dog based on nutritional levels established by the Association of American Feed Control Officials. The statement also indicates the life stage (e.g., growth/lactation, maintenance, or all life stages) for which the food is intended.
- **Manufacturer's contact information:** The name and address of the manufacturer, packer, or distributor are required. Sometimes manufacturers include a toll-free phone number or a website, but this information isn't mandatory.

FEEDING ALTERNATIVE DIETS

Although the common types of canine diets contain everything your dog needs to thrive, some people are looking at alternatives. Home-cooked diets allow Border Collie owners to have more control over what they feed their pets, while frozen and dehydrated diets offer a convenient solution for dog owners who want to feed their pets homemade food but don't have the time to prepare the meals.

Homemade diets are meals made from scratch. People who cook for their dogs must be sure to include a protein source (such as cooked chicken or beef), a carbohydrate source (such as potatoes or rice), and dog-safe vegetables or fruits for vitamins and minerals. Preparing homemade meals can be relatively simple, as long as you include all of the nutrients that your Border Collie needs. It's best to discuss homemade diets with your veterinarian to get his or her recommendations and to find out if you should add any supplements.

Dehydrated diets are designed to be complete and balanced, just like kibble or canned food. Dehydrated foods come in a powdered form—all you need to do is add water (and any extra veggies or meat, if desired) and mix. Besides giving your Border Collie a delicious and nutritious meal, you're also using less packaging and producing less garbage. Many dehydrated formulas are made with all-natural or organic ingredients.

Frozen meals can be a convenient way for you to give your Border Collie a homemade diet without all of the work. Gaining in popularity, these meals come ready to serve in your pet-supply store's frozen-food case.

If you're going to feed your Border Collie one of these alternative diets, first and foremost, visit a veterinarian. You may want to consult a veterinary nutritionist to help you develop a diet for your Border Collie, or you may want to visit a holistic vet after talking to your regular vet to get both of their advice.

Did You Know? If you think your Border Collie is looking a little pudgy, give him the "rib test." Gently run your hands down your dog's sides. What do you feel? If his ribs feel like the tops of your knuckles, he's too thin. If his sides feel soft, like the inside ball of your thumb, he's too fat. If his ribs feel like the tops of your closed fingers, he's just right.

Helpful Hints

No Thanks!

Though a diet rich in vegetables and fruits provides a cornucopia of vitamins, minerals, antioxidants, and phytonutrients, certain ingredients can poison dogs, leading to stomach upset or toxic reactions that could be fatal:

- **Avocado:** can cause stomach irritation
- **Onions:** can cause stomach irritation
- **Garlic:** in large enough amounts, can cause stomach irritation
- **Chocolate:** contains caffeine-like compounds that can cause vomiting, diarrhea, heart palpitations, tremors, seizures, and even death
- **Macadamia nuts:** can cause stomach upset and weakness,

as well as temporary paralysis
- **Grapes:** can cause kidney failure
- **Raisins:** can cause kidney failure
- **Artificial sweeteners:** can send animal into a hyperglycemic state and cause coma

TREATS FOR YOUR BORDER COLLIE

Treats come in all sizes and flavors, from crunchy biscuits to bakery-inspired doggy cookies to freeze-dried lamb and beef jerky. You can find treats in pet-supply stores and trendy dog bakeries across the country, or you can give your Border Collie safe human foods, such as pieces of hot dog, chunks of cheese, or slices of raw carrot.

You can feed your Border Collie treats to reward him for good behavior or simply to give him a special "extra" now and then. It's a pleasure to see your pup enjoying a delicious snack. Like all food, though, treats contain calories. Treats, whether those made for dogs or small pieces of healthy human food, should be factored into your dog's overall food intake, accounting for about 10 percent of his daily calories. Packaged treats should come with feeding guidelines for you to follow based on your dog's size.

After playing at the dog park, working on the farm, hiking on a trail, or practicing agility, your Border Collie's feathered locks—not to mention his nails, eyes, ears, and teeth—will need some attention. To ensure your dog's good health and good looks, plan to incorporate daily, weekly, and semi-monthly grooming rituals into your routine; doing so will enable you to maintain your Border Collie's appearance and check him over for injuries.

Grooming may sound like a lot of responsibility, but after becoming familiar with the handling, the tools, and the processes, grooming time will be a pleasurable experience for you and your Border Collie, resulting in a strong bond between the two of you and a nice-smelling dog whose good looks match his good behavior.

Grooming your Border Collie involves caring for his skin and coat, keeping his nails trimmed, cleaning his ears and around his eyes, and brushing his teeth. Though this working dog has a full coat of

Did You Know?

All dogs, Border Collies included, thrive on routines, so make the grooming process as consistent as possible. For instance, begin with brushing, then clip his toenails, and then brush his teeth—and follow the same routine every time so your dog knows what to expect from his grooming sessions.

abundant fur, he can be easily groomed at home with the right tools, a little instruction, and a short amount of time each day.

Before you start grooming, you must first choose a specific location as your grooming area. Always grooming in the same location will teach your dog what to expect and how to behave while you're grooming him. Some people use the bathroom and bathtub; some use an outdoor basin for bathing; others use a proper grooming table, like the ones that professional groomers use. Whatever you choose as your grooming zone, always put a nonslip pad or towel on the surface to prevent slippery paws from sliding.

You'll also need to have your grooming tools organized and close at hand in your grooming area. The supplies that follow can all be found at your local pet-supply store, through online pet-supply retailers, or through your groomer.

Shampoo and conditioner: Choose products formulated for adult dogs (or puppies, if your Border Collie is less than a year old). Avoid the shampoo-conditioner combos. They may cut bath time in half, but they don't get the coat as clean.

Blow dryer: You can find different varieties made for pets, including hands-free standing models. Make sure that the dryer has a low or cool setting, and the quieter it is, the better.

Comb: Purchase a quality metal or stainless-steel comb with long teeth. The type with narrow teeth on one end and wider teeth on the other will give you more combing options, such as for the fine hair between the pup's ears or for pulling out dead undercoat.

Slicker brush: These flat-backed tools effectively remove dead hair, tangles, and dirt (and the occasional bur or twig) from a dog's coat. Stash a few around the house so you can grab one for some spot brushing when you notice that your Border Collie needs it.

Bristle brush: Resembling a human hairbrush, this type of brush is used all over your dog's body. Choose one with bristles that are stiff enough to pass through your Border Collie's fur.

De-matter: From time to time, you will need to

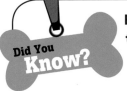
Did You Know?

Burs, twigs, and other outdoor debris are inevitable frustrations in Border Collie coats. Brush or pick them out as soon as possible. To coax out stubborn pieces, spray the area with conditioning spray and carefully remove them with your comb.

The Border Collie is a natural beauty who doesn't require complicated grooming, just routine maintenance.

use this device to pull out mats from your Border Collie's coat. This tool has several curved blades that are sharp on one side.

Scissors: Small scissors are used for trimming the hair around your Border Collie's ears, on the bottom of the feet around the foot pads, and around the anus. Select small-blade scissors that fit your hand comfortably.

Nail clippers: The two basic types are the scissor and the guillotine. Purchase whichever you're most comfortable with.

Styptic powder: Styptic powder, which stops the flow of blood, is good to have on hand in case of unexpected nail-trimming accidents.

Cotton balls: You'll use these for cleaning your Border Collie's ears and around his eyes.

Toothbrush and dog toothpaste: A child's soft toothbrush or a doggy toothbrush with some toothpaste made for dogs will keep your Border Collie's teeth tartar-free.

Towels: Keep a supply of dry towels on hand to sop up spills and dry off your clean dog.

Keep your grooming gear in a plastic bin or cardboard box for easy access; restock supplies as necessary.

Border Collies have sensitive skin, so take extra care when grooming. Brush your dog gently, massaging his coat with care. Keep an eye out for signs of allergic reactions to flea or insect bites, and choose a calming shampoo, such as an all-natural variety made with oatmeal, to soothe itchy skin.

CARING FOR THE COAT AND SKIN

The Border Collie is a double-coated breed, which means that your dog has a thick undercoat to keep him warm and an outer coat to repel water, burs, and twigs. He will shed (lose dead hairs) all year long, so you will want to brush him regularly to control loose hair, prevent tangling, remove debris, and keep his coat looking shiny and healthy.

Oils from the sebaceous glands under the skin naturally condition the dog's hair and skin. Shampooing too frequently with harsh products can cause dry, flaky skin; daily brushing releases the oils, keeps the skin and coat healthy, and prevents tangles and mats from forming.

Brushing How-To

If possible, brush your dog daily or even several times a day, if needed. To begin, get your Border Collie settled in your designated grooming spot. Use a comb and your fingers to gently loosen any tangles and remove debris. If a tangle proves difficult to comb out, spray it with some conditioner and continue working on it. Stubborn tangles can lead to mats, and if they're close to the skin, they can cause painful sores and infections if not dealt with. Mats that can't be untangled should be carefully removed with small scissors, taking care not to pull at your Border Collie's sensitive skin.

Once the coat is knot- and tangle-free, brush your Border Collie in sections using the slicker brush. Portion off a section of the coat with your hand and brush through it, starting near the skin and working out to the ends, until you can brush through the section with no resistance. Then move to the next section. It doesn't matter if you start at the front or the back of the dog, but

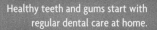
Healthy teeth and gums start with regular dental care at home.

NOTABLE & QUOTABLE

When you're looking for a groomer, look at personality. The groomer has to have a gentle disposition and rapport with dogs. The groomer should know how to handle the dog firmly but gently. And look for someone who has some credentials and experience.

—Debbie Slocum, a nationally certified master groomer and owner of Slocum Ridge Pet Camp in Glencoe, Alabama

don't forget the hair on the abdomen and chest. These areas are most vulnerable to tangles and mats.

After you can brush smoothly through the entire coat with the slicker brush, give your dog an all-over brushing with the bristle brush, working from root to tip and being careful not to scrape the skin. This stimulates oil production, encourages hair growth, and removes any loose hairs.

Rub-a-Dub-Dub

Your Border Collie will require a bath once or twice a month. Any more than that will dry out his sensitive skin and cause dandruff and brittle hair. Before bath time, gather all of the gear you'll need to wash, dry, and comb out your dog. You'll need shampoo, conditioner, a couple of fluffy towels, cotton balls, a comb, a slicker brush, and a blow dryer.

Did You Know? **Many breeders ready their pups for the grooming ritual when they're still very young by holding the pups, coddling them, peeking into their mouths, handling their paws, and inspecting their eyes and ears.** Most likely, by the time you meet your Border Collie, he will be used to being handled. You can continue the breeder's work by handling your Border Collie puppy every day, even if you aren't grooming him. Your dog needs to feel comfortable with someone touching his body, inspecting his eyes and ears, tickling his toes, and even rubbing his gums.

First, brush out your Border Collie's coat thoroughly. Tangles and mats will only tighten up and worsen in the tub.

Next, prepare the bathing area. For ease, many Border Collie owners use the bathtub or an outdoor water basin with a nonslip mat in the bottom. Gently plug your Border Collie's ears with cotton balls and lead him into the tub.

Wet your dog's head and body with lukewarm water, being careful not to get water in his ears. A pullout nozzle or hand-held sprayer attached to the faucet makes this job easy. Once your Border Collie is thoroughly wet, turn off the water. Using a quarter-sized drop of shampoo, wash and massage your dog's coat and skin, including his ears, underside, and rear. Do not get the shampoo near his eyes. Rinse out the soap completely, working from his head down his back and underneath his body. Once your dog is fully rinsed, apply the conditioner according to the manufacturer's instructions. Let it soak in, and then rinse it out thoroughly.

In warm weather, a thorough rubdown with a clean, dry towel will dry his coat. If the weather is chilly, don't let your Border Collie air-dry after his bath; he could catch a cold. Instead, wrap your clean dog in a big fluffy towel to soak up the excess water and then move on to the hair dryer on a low setting.

Lay your Border Collie on his side and begin blow-drying his hair. Use the lowest setting possible, keeping the dryer at least 8 inches from your dog's body to prevent scalding. With the dryer in one hand and a bristle brush in the other, dry your dog's abdomen, chest, and leg areas while brushing. When one side is dry, have him lie on his other side and repeat the process. Finally, stand him up

An active outdoor lifestyle can mean a coat that gets dirty often.

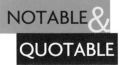

NOTABLE & QUOTABLE

A dog senses every energy from a person, so if you're nervous about cutting your dog's nails, he'll sense that. Do everything you can to feel comfortable and confident [during grooming].

—Shannan Madsen, a national certified master groomer at
Dales Town & Country in Surprise, Arizona

If your Border Collie gets skunked—and it's likely that he will at some point—try this recipe to remove the stench. Mix one quart of regular 3-percent hydrogen peroxide in a bucket with ¼ cup of baking soda. The mixture will fizz and bubble like a science experiment. Add a teaspoon of liquid soap or dishwashing detergent to help the mixture stick to your dog's coat. Wet the dog thoroughly with the mixture, being very careful around his face, and then rinse him with water or bathe him with shampoo and water.

and brush and dry the outer layers of the coat from the roots to the tips. Finish your Border Collie's bathing session with a thorough combing.

CARING FOR NAILS

Nail trimming should be done about once a month or more often as needed. You'll know that your Border Collie's nails have grown too long if you hear them clicking when he walks across the floor. An ideal time to trim your Border Collie's nails is after his bath when his nails are softened from the water, but any time will do.

All dogs' toenails grow continually and need to be trimmed to stay at a healthy length. If the nails grow too far past the pads of the feet, they could curve inward and cut into the pads. Long nails can also cause the dog to lose traction, as they could prevent the foot pads from hitting the ground. Long nails can tear upholstery, snag clothing, and cause scratches, too.

You can choose from several types of nail trimmers made for dogs at your local pet-supply store. Whichever style you choose, select the right size for your Border Collie's nails.

When you trim your dog's nails for the first few times, enlist the help of another person to steady your Border Collie. Having an extra set of hands will be very helpful when your dog starts squirming. You can position your Border Collie in a number of ways: held against your chest, standing on a table or other nonslip surface, or lying on his back. Choose a position that's comfortable for you and your dog.

With the dog held securely in place by your assistant, hold the trimmers with your dominant hand and the dog's paw with the other hand. Start with one nail. Gently press the toe between your index finger and your thumb, which will extend the nail and prevent it from retracting. Only clip off the portion of the nail that's curving downward. If you're nervous about cutting into the quick (the blood vessel that runs through each nail), clip only the very tip. Have some styptic powder nearby, just in case you do nick the quick and need to stop the bleeding. With time, trimming your Border Collie's nails will become second nature to both you and the dog.

In addition to trimming your Border Collie's nails, you'll also want to trim the hair on the feet that grows between the dog's pads and toes. This hair can pick up dirt and debris, causing mats to form. Simply trim the hair carefully with a pair of small scissors.

THOSE PEARLY WHITES

Dental hygiene is an extremely important part of your Border Collie's grooming routine. Bacteria buildup from poor oral health has been linked to infection and disease in

dogs' major organs, including their hearts, livers, and kidneys.

Plaque (which is made up of billions of bacteria) builds up quickly, resulting in tartar buildup, gingivitis, and bad breath. The dog's gums become swollen and irritated and, in extreme instances, bleed and fill with pus. If left untreated, periodontal disease could set in, and the dog may need to have teeth pulled. All of this can be prevented by establishing and maintaining good doggy dental-care habits at home.

Your Border Collie's teeth should be brushed several times a week using a soft-bristled toothbrush and toothpaste made especially for dogs, not for humans. Human toothpaste is not safe for your Border Collie, and he probably won't like the taste of it anyway.

Brushing will remove tartar and break up any plaque. You can use a child's toothbrush or a toothbrush made for a dog, but if your Border Collie doesn't like the toothbrush, try massaging his teeth and gums with some of the toothpaste on your finger to get him used to the procedure.

When brushing your dog's teeth, use a circular motion, just as you do on your own teeth. Clean the outside and the inside of each tooth, and don't miss those teeth in the back of the mouth, where plaque and tartar tend to accumulate the most.

If your Border Collie refuses to cooperate, you may choose to use one of the dental gels currently available through veterinarians and pet-supply stores. Simply apply the solution to the dog's canine teeth, and his saliva and tongue action will spread it around his mouth. The gel protects the teeth, preventing plaque from building up and tartar from forming.

In addition to brushing, offer your Border Collie crunchy treats designed to break down tartar and plaque. Feeding your Border Collie dry food can also help scrape off plaque that builds up on the teeth, but there is no substitute for actually brushing your dog's chompers.

Border Collies who aren't eating, drinking, or playing with their favorite chew toys as they usually do may be suffering from gum disease. Look at your dog's teeth and gums and call your veterinarian if you suspect that something is wrong. In some cases, your veterinarian must anesthetize the dog to clean a neglected mouth. Just like surgery, this procedure has risks, so avoid it by maintaining your Border Collie's oral health and visiting your veterinarian regularly.

EAR AND EYE CARE

A Border Collie's ears stand erect or semi-erect, which leaves them open to dirt, grime, and even ear mites. When your Border Collie plays in the yard or herds sheep, his ears are vulnerable to all sorts of debris. Cleaning your dog's ears several times a week will keep them healthy.

Start by gently inspecting your Border Collie's ears. Gently hold the edge of each

When trimming your dog's nails, be careful not to hit the quick, which is the vein inside the nail. Clipping the quick is painful and can cause your Border Collie's nail to bleed. To find the quick, use a flashlight or look at the outside of your dog's nails—you should be able to see the opaque portion in the center base of the nail; that's the quick.

it's a Fact

Chewing on sturdy toys can help keep a dog's teeth free of tartar and plaque.

ear and check for wax, discharge, odor, or signs of ear mites. A moderate amount of wax is normal, but any discharge or odor could signal a problem, such as an ear infection. Monitor the situation and consult your veterinarian if it persists.

Using a cotton ball moistened with ear-cleaning solution, wipe the inside of the ear, getting inside all the folds and creases. Use a fresh cotton ball for the other ear. Dry the ears thoroughly, using a clean cotton ball for each. Avoid cotton swabs, as they can damage the inner ear if used incorrectly.

If you see dark brown or black debris on the cotton ball, or if you see your dog shaking his head or scratching at his ears. your Border Collie might have ear mites, which thrive on ear wax and other matter in the ear canal. Wipe each ear until the cotton ball comes out clean, and do it daily. If symp-toms persist, talk to your veterinarian about over-the-counter or prescription ear-mite remedies.

Your Border Collie's eyes need minimal attention, but they shouldn't be ignored. If goop collects around the corners of his eyes, wipe them gently with a clean rag moistened with warm water. Also watch for eye infections caused by foxtails or debris getting into the dog's tear ducts.

Tear stains, which appear as red or brown stains on the fur around a dog's eyes, may occur if something is irritating the eyes and causing them to water excessively. To control the staining, first identify and remove the source of the irritation. Wipe the eye area daily with a cotton ball dipped in a safe eye-cleansing solution. There are also diet supplements designed to eliminate tear stains, but they can take weeks to work.

Questions for the Groomer

Even if you choose to use a professional groomer, you'll still be responsible for the routine maintenance tasks of daily brushing, dental care, and cleaning eyes and ears as needed. Before you choose a groomer and drop off your dog for that first grooming session, you should examine the shop and meet the person who will be working with your dog. As you're checking out the facility, make sure that it is clean and well maintained, and take notice of how the staff is handling any dogs there at the time. Also ask the owner or manager the following questions:

1. Do you require proof of vaccinations, including kennel cough? Dogs with communicable diseases should not be allowed in the shop.
2. What kind of hair dryers do you use? Grooming shops will typically use free-standing or cage dryers. Responsible groomers use the type that turn off if they get too hot, or they will hand-dry the dogs instead.
3. What kind of training have you and your staff had? Though certification is not mandated at this time, a groomer can earn documented proof of passing a practical skills assessment and a written exam.
4. How much experience do you and your staff have? The more experience, the better.
5. Do you and your staff have experience with Border Collies? Ideally, the groomer has worked with your breed before.
6. What kinds of products do you use on the dogs? The breeder should explain why he or she chooses specific products for your dog's coat.
7. How do you restrain unruly dogs? The dogs' safety should always be the first priority.
8. Do you have any references? Reputable groomers will have many satisfied clients.
9. Are you insured and bonded? This gives you added confidence in leaving your dog with the groomer.
10. What hours are you open? Do you offer after-hours or weekend appointments? You'll need to find a groomer whose hours fit your schedule.

You should feel extremely comfortable with your groomer, as he or she is responsible for your Border Collie's safety and well-being when your dog is at the salon.

AN OBEDIENT

Every year, millions of dog owners relinquish dogs to shelters because of their pets' perceived bad behavior. Well-meaning people adopt puppies with every intention of teaching them basic manners and obedience, reinforcing training throughout their lives, and raising adult dogs that can work and play right alongside them. Unfortunately, many times those good intentions fall by the wayside, especially when the puppy starts to chew through drywall or rip the stuffing from couch cushions. Before long, the adorable pup finds himself sequestered in the garage or living in the backyard or barn, eventually ending up in the local pound or humane society.

The good news is that it doesn't have to be this way. Training any dog is about teaching him what behavior is allowed and what is forbidden, which means that

Remember that your Border Collie will learn what to do—and what not to do—quickly. If you're not careful with your timing and how you issue your cues, you could be teaching your pup to respond to signals that you're not even aware of. Be cognizant of what you're doing during training and be consistent with your cues, and your Border Collie will respond how you want him to.

it's a **Fact**

you, the owner, will have to be decisive about the things that you permit and prohibit. When both you and your dog understand the boundaries, your Border Collie will easily become a valued member of your family for a lifetime.

A SOLID FOUNDATION

When you train your Border Collie puppy to follow your cues, you're setting up a foundation for your future relationship, whether you intend to work him, compete with him, or simply have him join you in your favorite activities. Your dog will learn to respect you—his leader—and obey your cues. He will learn how to behave around other people, with other critters, and in different situations. He will learn to do exactly what you expect him to do with one meaningful word or whistle. All it takes is a solid foundation of training in basic obedience.

First and foremost, training your Border Collie teaches him the hierarchy of your household. When you (and everyone in the household) issue consistent cues and expect the pup to obey them, he's learning that humans are in charge. This critical step in your Border Collie's cognitive development will prevent him from walking all over you later. As a highly intelligent dog, your Border Collie will push the limits, so it's up to you to set the parameters and make your expectations clear early on in your relationship.

Training your Border Collie also makes him enjoyable for others to be around. This breed loves trips to the dog park, a few laps around the agility ring, and hikes down his favorite trail, and with a well-trained Border Collie, you'll be able to enjoy out-and-about adventures with no concern of him barking, bolting, or being destructive.

People will enjoy coming to your home and playing with your pup much more if he's not herding them, nipping at their heels, or growling at them.

Another reason to train your Border Collie to obey the rules is to keep him safe. For example, if you're outside and your dog runs off, he will return at your call if trained. The untrained Border Collie may keep running and could hurt himself, become lost, or worse. If you're walking through a crowd and you've taught your Border Collie to heel, he won't pull on the leash or get into trouble.

If you plan to train your dog to work livestock, obedience plays an even greater role—especially if he's charged with herding a few dozen head of sheep! A Border Collie may instinctively know what to do in a working situation, but he'll need to learn to take direction from you rather than make decisions on his own.

Many people may think of their dogs as their "kids," and all kids need to learn the rules of proper behavior. In this chapter, you'll learn what you need to know about socialization, the different types of training, and obedience basics.

PUP MEET WORLD

Socialization, or teaching your Border Collie how to behave in social situations, is one of the most critical things you can do to ensure a well-mannered dog. As soon as your puppy or new dog comes home, you should begin to expose him to a variety of people, animals, sights, sounds, and circumstances so that he understands that these things are not threats. A well-socialized dog is confident. He won't be afraid of loud noises or shy away from unfamiliar faces, and he will get along with other dogs, pets, and livestock.

The best way to get your Border Collie well socialized is to introduce him to different kinds of people and situations. Have him meet a man with a beard, take him to a dog-friendly restaurant, take him for a ride in the car. Go online to download a socialization checklist at **DogChannel.com/Club-Border.**

A get-together at your home is an opportunity for your Border Collie to meet and greet a houseful of people in an environment that he considers safe and cozy. Ask your friends to arrive wearing various garb, such as hats, beards, uniforms, and costumes. Encourage them to interact positively with the pup and make sure that everyone gets the chance to hold and pet him at least once.

ENGAGE HIS SENSES

When your pup is between three and twelve weeks old, he will turn his attention from his littermates to his human caretakers. At this time in his life, the breeder will start to introduce the puppies to different people. People should touch, hold, and pet the youngsters, gently tickling their toes and handling their ears. Rough games, chasing, or tug-of-war could lead to behavior issues down the road and should be avoided. The breeder will make sure that the puppies' socialization experiences are as positive as possible; rather than introducing the pups to a roomful of rambunctious children, for instance, the breeder will have the pups spend some time with one or two well-behaved children in a supervised environment. People of all ages, both genders, and various ethnicities and backgrounds should meet the puppies; this way, when your Border Collie comes home with you, he will be familiar with all types of people.

When your Border Collie comes home at about twelve weeks old, you should continue to socialize him. Between the ages of twelve and twenty weeks, your puppy is most receptive to learning how to handle new sounds, smells, and sights. This is the best time to socialize him to different environments. Put your Border Collie on a leash and take him for a walk through the park. Let him smell the grass, hear the sounds of traffic, and meet people on the street. Introduce him to the places you frequent. Carefully introduce the world to your Border Collie in brief, monitored bursts until he feels comfortable. Week by week, you can provide new experiences to help stimulate and socialize your pet.

As soon as your puppy has been fully vaccinated (after about sixteen weeks), you can start introducing him to other animals, too. Get together with owners of well-behaved dogs to organize play dates and other supervised meetings between your Border Collie and their dogs. Puppy kindergarten classes are also excellent for socialization. Your pup should be introduced to other types of animals, including cats, rabbits, and sheep and other livestock—always under your watchful eye, of course.

FEAR NOT!

At around two months, four months, and twelve to fourteen months of age, dogs go through imprint periods during which they are more likely to fear things around them. During these fear periods, do your best to prevent scary things from happening and to avoid exposing your pup to situations that he may find stressful or frightening. Being highly sensitive dogs, Border Collies are easily spooked by loud noises, such as thunderclaps and fireworks. Some noises or situations, such as thunderstorms, are unavoidable, but others can be prevented. For example, wait to run the vacuum until your pup is out playing Frisbee with your son, or perhaps decide not to host that crazy Super Bowl party this year.

In addition to going through fear periods, your pup will miss the comfort and familiarity of his mother and littermates when he comes home with you.

When your pup goes through his fear phases, here are some ways to handle his fright:

- **Distract him:** If something frightens your Border Collie, don't try to hold him and calm him, as this could actually encourage his fearful behavior. Instead, redirect his attention to his ball or a treat, saying, "What's this?" The key is to make your dog think about something else.
- **Watch your tone:** When your pup seems fearful of something, speak to him in a calm, matter-of-fact tone or in a high-pitched, fun tone, both of which will help distract your dog from his anxieties. Resist the urge to use a soothing tone, which could be mistaken as sympathy and thus only reinforce his fears.
- **Investigate the scary item:** If possible, walk over to whatever spooked your pup, Touch it and show him that it's not as frightening as he thought, saying in a calm voice, "Look, it's not scary."
- **Don't force him:** Sometimes, your pup won't want anything to do with the scary item, and that's okay. When he's ready, he'll approach it on his own. If you force the situation, you may make the fear worse.
- **Ask your vet:** If other techniques aren't working, overly anxious dogs may benefit from herbal or prescription calmatives, which your vet can recommend.

To keep your Border Collie well socialized and not fearful, you must continue introducing him to new people, circumstances, and creatures throughout his life. Regular walks around the neighborhood and visits to herding or agility trials are good ways to socialize, as are trips to friends' houses, the beach, or the pet-supply store. Continually exposing your Border Collie to different places and experiences will keep him socialized and sound.

SCHOOL DAYS

Many different training theories and practices exist today. Trainers use varying approaches to teach dogs how to behave: some use a balanced method that incorporates positive reinforcement and correction; others use a behavior-driven approach; and still others use clicker-based training, which uses a clicking noise as a reward. Clicker training teaches your Border Collie to respond to something meaningless—a click—by associating it with something

Collars come in a variety of styles. A buckle collar is typically made of nylon or leather and has a buckle. A slip collar is a length of chain or rope with rings on either end. The chain or rope is pulled through one of the rings to form a loop that's slipped over the dog's head. A martingale collar is usually made of nylon and has two loops: a small loop, called the "control loop," which causes the collar to tighten if the dog pulls on the leash; and a larger loop, called an "adjustment loop," that goes around the dog's neck. Choose the collar that works best for you when training your Border Collie.

it's a **Fact**

valuable, such as food or a favorite toy. Through conditioning, the dog eventually responds to the click with the enthusiasm normally reserved for tasty morsels. The advantage of clicker training is that you can reinforce desired behavior at almost the exact moment that the behavior occurs.

One aspect that all successful and humane training methods have in common is positive reinforcement. Positive reinforcement rewards good behavior with properly timed treats, praise, and lots of love, which makes the dog want to obey you, because he knows that good things will follow.

You should start learning about training before your Border Collie comes home. Educate yourself by reading books dedicated to positive training techniques and canine behavior. If you are a more visual learner, there are plenty of other types of media on the market, including DVDs and online tutorials, that will help you with step-by-step training.

In addition to your own education and edification, your pup will need to hit the books, too—in the form of a training class. As soon as your new Border Collie, puppy or adult, bounds through the door, training should begin. You can enroll your youngster in puppy kindergarten classes when he is about ten to twelve weeks old. In most cases, puppies have to complete at least two rounds of vaccinations to be allowed to participate. Basic *sit*, *down*, *stay*, and *come* cues are taught by an instructor who understands the short attention spans of puppies. Not only will your Border Collie learn some basic commands, but he will also have the important opportunity to socialize with other dogs.

Basic obedience training courses are for older dogs, four months of age or older, who have graduated from puppy kindergarten.

With the proper training, your Border Collie will be as well behaved as he is beautiful. One certification that all dogs should receive is the American Kennel Club's Canine Good Citizen (CGC), which rewards dogs who demonstrate good manners. Go to **DogChannel.com/Club-Border** and click on "Downloads" to learn about the ten exercises required for your dog to be a CGC.

JOIN OUR ONLINE **Club Border**™

Dog treats range from biscuits and bone-shaped cookies to gourmet baked delights made just for dogs. These types of treats, however, are not designed for training, as they're too big and take too long to eat. When you're training your dog, most experts recommend offering small, chopped-up pieces of real meat or cheese (such as hot dogs, dehydrated liver, or cheddar) that can be popped into your dog's mouth and chewed quickly, thus providing an instant reward. The protein is healthy for your pet, and the smaller bites won't add too many calories to your Border Collie's diet.

Basic commands are taught and reinforced, and the instructor will also go over some problem-solving tips for behaviors such as digging, barking, and chewing.

An alternative to training classes is to have a private trainer come to your home. Private training is done one-on-one and can be individualized to fit your Border Collie's needs and your schedule. This type of training is often the best option for a dog with behavior problems.

You can find training classes and private trainers through your veterinarian, your breeder, your breed club, your local humane society, and even your favorite pet-supply store. Trainers can be found online and in the phone book, but personal references often make finding a good trainer easier.

Whether you choose to train your Border Collie yourself, enroll him in classes, or enlist the help of a private trainer, your dog will need to learn how to understand and obey specific cues. Let's take a closer look at the most basic cues, which build a firm foundation for good behavior.

These cues only scratch the surface of what's possible with your Border Collie. After learning these basic exercises, he'll be ready for some on-the-job training and will become a well-behaved companion and sidekick in no time!

LEARNING THE CUES

Obeying basic cues will keep your Border Collie safe and well behaved at home and in public. Before you begin, gather some treats, such as small pieces of dehydrated meat or cheese. Attach your Border Collie's collar or harness to a 4-foot leash and lead him to an area with few distractions and where you'll have plenty of room to work. Plan to dedicate about twenty minutes a day to your training sessions, but practice the cues constantly in your day-to-day activities. Encourage your family members to do the same, staying consistent with the cues that they use and the timing of their rewards. Practice will help your dog learn that obeying your cues brings rewards in the form of treats and your attention.

The Recall or *Come* Cue

This is one of the most important cues for your dog to master. Your Border Collie should learn to come to you immediately the first time you call him. Learning to obey this cue will keep your dog out of danger.

Teaching your Border Collie to respond to his name when you say it is the beginning of the recall, or *come*, cue. Stand in front of your dog and say his name in a fun, upbeat voice. When he looks at you, reward him with a treat and lots of praise. Practice this for a few days before you begin training, and before long, when your

NOTABLE & QUOTABLE *Training should start immediately, from day one. When puppies are that young, they're little sponges. They like to follow you around, they like to look up at you, they're curious, and they want to be with you. When they hit that adolescent age—five to eighteen months old—you get a little bit of the teenager thing. If I have the opportunity to capture them when they're young, I'll immediately train everything and lay a great foundation.*

—Kathy Santo, president of Everyday Pets and dog trainer in Ramsey, New Jersey

You want your Border Collie to come running whenever you call him.

Border Collie hears his name, he will look at you and wait for something to happen.

At this point, you can introduce the verbal cue "Come." Start with your Border Collie on leash, and have the leash folded in your hand so that he's just a short distance from you. Using a treat as a lure, say, "Rudy, come," and walk backward, which will cause your dog to follow you. Reward and praise him when he reaches you.

When he has proven himself reliable at a short distance, let out a little more of the leash's length and repeat the exercise. Over the course of your training sessions, progress to longer distances and eventually to a longer leash. You can practice from 20 to 30 feet away with a leash or long line.

Once your dog is reliable on leash, you can begin practicing off leash in a safely fenced area, starting over from a short distance and gradually progressing to longer distances. Before long, your Border Collie will run directly to you every time you call him to come, no matter where he is or what he is doing.

Sit

The *sit* cue teaches your dog to hold still while in a sitting position. A very important lesson in self-control, it's likely the first

cue your Border Collie will learn. This cue is the cornerstone of many other exercises that you will teach your Border Collie.

Stand in front of your dog, holding a treat in one hand. Bend at the waist and hold the treat over the dog's nose. Say in a firm voice, "Rudy, sit." As you say those words, move the treat up and back over his head, toward his tail. The dog will look up to follow the treat with his eyes, which will cause him to lower his rear into a seated position. Praise him with "Good dog," and immediately reward him with a treat when his back end hits the ground.

After several training sessions, your Border Collie will know what's expected of him when he hears the verbal cue "Sit," and you'll no longer have to move the treat to lure him into the *sit* position. Even after you eliminate the hand motion, still keep up the praise and rewards when he assumes the *sit* position, as this will reinforce the meaning of the cue and let your Border Collie know that he is doing what you want him to do.

Down

The *down* cue teaches your dog to lie down and remain in place; this is a critical behavior in the Border Collie's line of work.

A well-trained Border Collie respects you as his leader, responds to cues, and is socialized to a variety of people, other animals, and situations.

You can use this cue when you want your Border Collie to relax on his bed or freeze in the field when the sheep seem spooked.

Begin by telling your dog to sit. Then, holding a treat in front of his nose, say, "Rudy, down," and move the treat to the floor between his paws. Move the treat back toward you along the floor; as his nose follows the treat and he lies down, praise him and give him the treat. The *down* may take a little while longer for your Border Collie to learn than the *sit*, as not all dogs are initially at ease in the *down* position.

Stay

The *stay* cue, used with both the *sit* and the *down* cues, trains your Border Collie to stay in place until you release him. The *sit/stay* cue is for shorter periods of time; the *down/stay* cue is for longer periods.

Start by facing your dog and telling him to sit. With your open palm facing his nose, say, "Rudy, stay." Slowly take one step backward and stay there. If your Border Collie stays in place, go back to him after a few seconds and reward him with treats and praise. Gradually increase your distance from the dog and the length of time you expect him to stay. Keep lavishing the praise and giving a treat reward with each successful exercise. Once he's reliable with the *sit/stay*, start over from the beginning with your dog in the *down* position.

During your training, if your dog fidgets and gets up to come to you when you step backward, enlist the help of a friend or relative who can hold your Border Collie's leash to keep him in place after you give the *stay* cue.

Heel

Teaching your Border Collie to heel (walk nicely by your side) makes taking a walk on leash a fun and enjoyable experience for both of you.

To teach your Border Collie to heel, connect the leash to your dog's collar or harness and hold the leash in your hand. Stand in front of your dog, facing him. Have a handful of treats in your other hand, and show the dog the treats before you start walking. Begin to walk backward, moving the treat slowly in front of him as if you're leading him by the nose. Continue walking backward, all the while holding the treat where your dog can see it. As he follows you, praise him, and reward him with the treat when you stop walking.

When your dog follows you nicely in this fashion, you'll turn so that you and your dog are walking side by side, with your dog on your left side (traditionally, dogs walk on their handlers' left side in shows and other competitions). When you start walking side by side, lure your Border Collie with a treat so that he stays in step with you, neither pulling ahead nor lagging behind. Give the verbal cue "Heel" as you walk. As your dog gets the hang of walking next to you in the heel position, you can eliminate the treat lure, but keep up with the praise.

Leave It

You can teach your Border Collie to ignore something using the *leave it* cue. This command comes in handy if your dog likes to taste things that he shouldn't or if he decides that he wants to roll in something stinky. You want to teach him to leave things alone when told.

To teach your dog to leave it, ask him to sit and stay. Show him a tasty treat and place it in your hand, closing your hand around the treat. Have an even more desirable treat hidden in your other hand or in a pocket. Hold out the hand that's concealing the treat and say "Leave it." If your dog lunges for the morsel in your hand, grab his leash and tell him "No." When he stays in place or moves away from the treat, praise him in an upbeat voice and give him the other treat that you've been hiding.

Continue practicing *leave it* in different locations, using different kinds of treats. You can also practice when you see your Border Collie going for something that he shouldn't, such as the garbage can or food from the kitchen counter. Always reward him with a treat and praise when he obeys and turns his attention away from the forbidden object.

Part of being a well-mannered and obedient dog includes following the rules of the household, set forth by you. It's up to you to teach your Border Collie the correct way to act in the house, outside, in public places, and with other people and animals. Occasionally, though, problems can occur.

Some of the behaviors that we perceive as problems are actually quite natural to dogs; for example, dogs communicate by barking, and dogs chew to relieve discomfort when their puppy teeth fall out. When these behaviors become habits, or when they're done in an inappropriate or destructive manner, they need to be corrected.

DISCIPLINE

In the previous chapter, you discovered how to use positive reinforcement to teach your Border Collie basic commands, such as *sit* and *stay*. When you use corrections in training, you also use positive reinforcement, but you correct your dog when he

A veterinary behaviorist can provide professional assistance to owners who are unable to cope with unmanageable dogs. A canine behavioral therapist specializes in diagnosing and treating complex behavior issues that don't readily respond to conventional training methods.

it's a
Fact

SMART TIP! **Because of his penchant for herding, it's likely that your Border Collie may try to herd bicyclists or cars—and that's a very dangerous habit.** Many dogs learn to steer clear of cars only after a close call. By teaching your pup basic commands, such as down and come, you'll be better equipped to prevent something tragic from happening.

does something he shouldn't. You'll need to correct bad behavior and reinforce good behavior. You can do this in several ways, depending on the particular action that you're trying to correct.

Correction should never include physical punishment. Hitting or harming your Border Collie in any way is inhumane, and it can create an animal that fears people. Instead, correction involves getting your Border Collie's attention and stopping the unwanted behavior at that moment.

One tool that you'll use is your voice. The tone of your voice communicates emotion or feeling to your dog. An upbeat, high-pitched tone communicates happiness or excitement, while a lower-pitched, guttural tone communicates anger or sternness. Your Border Collie will respond to these sounds as he would to his mother or pack leader. When you're praising your dog for obeying the *sit* command, for example, you use a happy tone. Conversely, when you're correcting your dog for barking inappropriately, you use the low warning tone. You're not yelling at the dog, you're using a different tone of voice. This means that even a soft-spoken person can correct his or her dog effectively.

Another tool you'll need to master is consistency. If everyone who comes in contact with your Border Collie expects the same behavior from him, he won't be confused about how he should act.

Before you begin corrective training, however, check with your veterinarian. Some bad behavior, such as chronic house-soiling or chewing, can be caused by medical conditions. Other troublesome behaviors can be exacerbated by something in your Border Collie's diet or a lack of exercise. Get a clean bill of health and then begin training.

SOLVING PROBLEM BEHAVIORS

Border Collies can have their fair share of problem behaviors, many of which are tied to the breed's intelligence and activity level. As mentioned before, a bored Border Collie can and will get himself into trouble. Here's what you need to know to handle some of the most common canine challenges.

Speak in Turn

Dogs bark to communicate. From protecting their homes from strangers to trying to get their owners' attention, barking is a natural dog behavior. Guarding the home can be a positive reason to bark, and it's likely that your Border Collie will vocalize only when he needs to. If you have a barker, you'll want to determine why he is barking before you begin corrective training.

- Do you show your Border Collie attention every time he barks? If so, then he has trained you! He knows that if he barks, you'll come running.
- Does your dog bark when someone comes to the door? If so, he's protecting his territory.

If your Border Collie always has something to say, some training can help him learn when to be quiet.

- Does he bark when nobody's home? He may be suffering from separation anxiety.
- Does he bark when he's working or herding sheep? He's just doing his job.

After you've narrowed down some of the reasons for your dog's barking, you can start correcting his behavior.

First, when your Border Collie barks, don't yell at him. To your dog, yelling sounds like barking, and he'll think that you're trying to speak to him in his own language! Instead, ignore the barking. This may sound difficult, but if your dog realizes that he won't get any attention when he barks, he's more likely to stop the behavior. Reward him for not barking by saying, "Sparky, good quiet" in an upbeat voice.

Enlist a friend to come to your door and ring the doorbell. Allow your Border Collie a few warning barks and then tell him "Quiet." When he stops barking, say "Good quiet" and reinforce the quiet behavior with praise and a treat. Your dog will soon learn that staying quiet after he's done his job will earn him a reward.

You'll also want to practice the *quiet* cue in public. Grab some treats and put your Border Collie on leash. Walk to the park or someplace where he barks at people or dogs. Say "Quiet" and lavish him with praise and treats when he obeys.

it's a Fact

Male dogs initiate sexual behavior. A male will show interest in a female by sniffing at the female's nose, ears, neck, flank, and rump, and she'll do the same with him.

No Nipping or Biting

Many horrifying dog attacks have been reported in the media. Although these incidents tend to involve aggressive or poorly trained dogs, even a Border Collie needs be trained never to bare his teeth, never to touch his teeth to a person's skin or clothing, and never to bite. This is one of the most important lessons that you must teach your pet.

Mouthing is normal behavior in puppies. Between four and twelve weeks old, pups learn bite inhibition from their mother and littermates. They learn the amount of mouth pressure they can use without causing pain or harm as they play with their brothers and sisters. If a puppy is removed from his littermates before learning this inhibition, his human pack leader will have to teach him. Start "no bite" training as soon as possible to ensure that your dog's mouthing habit doesn't develop into something dangerous. Your Border Collie should know not to bite by the time he is eighteen weeks old.

When your puppy nips at you or bites you, or even just mouths you, say, "Sparky, no bite." Stop playing with him and walk away. Do not allow your dog to nip at your heels or chase your feet. This will teach him that biting and nipping result in the withdrawal of your attention.

If your Border Collie continues to use his mouth inappropriately, even after consistent training, discuss the situation with your veterinarian. He may be able to recommend a professional trainer or animal behaviorist to help you deal with the problem.

Chew on This

Chewing, like digging or barking, is something that dogs do. When they're between three and six months old, puppies begin

A Border Collie's typical herding behavior can include nipping to control the livestock.

teething, and with teething comes chewing. They will chew anything and everything. As their baby teeth fall out and their adult teeth erupt, chewing relieves their discomfort. Puppies go through a second chewing phase when they're between seven and nine months old as they explore their new territory.

Unfortunately, puppies develop a fondness for chewing during these phases once they find out how much fun chewing can be! It relieves tension and anxiety, and it makes their sore gums feel better. For adult dogs, chewing massages their gums and occupies their time.

Chewing the wrong things, however, can be destructive to your belongings and dangerous to your Border Collie. He can swallow something poisonous, or something small can get lodged in his throat.

Because chewing is just part of being a dog, your Border Collie should have his own things to chew on from the very beginning. Instead of waiting until the improper behavior starts, be proactive. Give him his own size-appropriate chew toys, such as hard rubber balls that you can stuff with treats, sturdy nylon bones, or durable rope tug toys. Limit his toys to a few at a time; you don't want your Border Collie to think that everything in sight is for his chewing pleasure.

To help your dog resist temptation, put away items that you don't want him to chew, especially those that can be harmful to him. Children's toys with small removable pieces that can be ingested, household cleaners and personal hygiene items, insect and rodent traps, electrical cords, and hobby supplies are just a few common household items that pose a danger to all dogs.

Praise your Border Collie often when he chews the right objects. If your dog finds something else to gnaw on, take the object away and give him one of his toys, saying "Good dog" when he takes it.

Don't Dig the Digging

Border Collies will dig. Some dogs dig to create a cool and cozy place to relax, and others dig to get out of a confined area. Instead of trying to teach your Border Collie not to dig, give him a specific place to dig. It will appease those digging tendencies, keep your dog occupied, and burn off some excess energy.

Choose a section of your yard and designate it your dog's digging area. Fill the area with loose dirt, making sure that it has no pesticides, sharp objects, or other dangers hidden within. Introduce your Border Collie to the digging area by bringing him over to it and placing a toy or a treat on the dirt. You can even bury a biscuit or two after he gets used to the area.

When you see your Border Collie digging in the right area, praise him with a "Good dog." If he digs in other places in the yard and you catch him in the act, move him to his digging area and praise him when he starts digging there. Fill in the other holes and, if you have to, lay some wire mesh over them to discourage further digging in forbidden places.

Four on the Floor

In Border Collie language, jumping up means "I'm a happy dog" and "Look at me!" Jumping up means that your dog wants to be the center of attention.

As hard as it may be, it's imperative not to acknowledge your Border Collie when he jumps up. Instead, tell him to sit. Only after he obeys should you pet him. Eventually he'll learn that to receive the attention he wants, he'll have to sit, not jump up.

Your Border Collie also needs to learn to sit for other people. Use the leash if you must, and when guests come to the door and your Border Collie jumps up, say "Sparky, no jump," followed by "Sparky, sit." Once the dog is sitting, allow your guests to praise him and give him the attention he wants.

Your Border Collie must learn that the only way he'll get attention is if he sits first, which means that every member of the family must ignore his jumping up consistently. Praise him lavishly every time he sits for attention or obeys your "No jump" cues. Soon, your dog will sit automatically before every greeting.

Accidents Happen

You've been taking your Border Collie puppy to his bathroom area regularly and letting him relieve himself after every meal, playtime, and nap. He's on his way to becoming house-trained. But then, he makes a mistake. What do you do?

Did You Know?

Dog-appeasing pheromones are unique chemical compounds that elicit calm in dogs. The pheromones, produced by lactating dams, activate the bonding process by triggering a sense of security in newborns. Dogs of any age instinctively respond to this scent. A synthetic form, found through your vet or at pet-supply stores, has been developed as a calming aid for our pet dogs.

Keep in mind that the act of going to the bathroom isn't the mistake; going in the wrong place is the problem. If you catch your pup in the act, use a corrective tone of voice to tell him "Sparky, no," and then immediately take him to his outdoor potty area and let him finish his business there. When he does, praise him and celebrate that he is going outside.

Clean the soiled area with white vinegar or an over-the-counter enzyme-based pet stain cleaner. Dogs tend to continue soiling in areas that smell like feces or urine, so removing all traces of the accident will prevent your dog from using that area again.

Don't correct your Border Collie after he makes a mistake—he won't understand the connection between the correction and the mistake he made hours (or even minutes) ago. Also, never rub your dog's face in the mess. It's not just an unnecessarily harsh punishment, but your dog will think that you are mad at him because he relieved himself, not because he did it in the wrong place. Instead, encourage and praise your dog even more when he does go in the correct bathroom area. Reinforcing the positive behavior is the best way to discourage the negative.

You'll also want to keep a close eye on your Border Collie. If you know where he is at all times, and you're watching him, you can stop an accident from happening. A circling and sniffing dog is a dog who's searching for a bathroom, so ask him in an upbeat voice, "Sparky, do you have to go potty?" If he doesn't run to the door on his own, lead him there or even carry him outside if you need to. Take him to his designated area and praise him when he goes.

Coprophagia

Feces eating, or coprophagia, is one of the most vile habits that your Border Collie can engage in, but, believe it or not, it is completely normal. Experts report that diets with low digestibility, containing relatively low levels of fiber and high levels of starch, increase the likelihood of coprophagia. Therefore, a high-fiber diet may decrease the chance that your Border Collie will engage in this dirty habit.

Though it is considered a normal canine behavior, coprophagia increases the risk that your pup will become infested with worms or other parasites that are passed through excrement.

To discourage feces eating, feed your Border Collie nutritionally complete food. If dietary changes don't do the trick and no medical cause can be found, you will have to modify the behavior through environmental changes before it becomes a habit.

You can try adding an unpalatable substance to the feces or, if he's eating his own poop, you can add something to his food that will make it unpleasant tasting

Did You Know?

Foraging is a normal canine behavior, but it becomes a nuisance when your dog is foraging through your garbage can or the pantry. Reprimanding him will likely just cause him to hunt for food behind your back—your brainy Border Collie will simply wait until the coast is clear before resuming his search. Block the kitchen with a gate or secure garbage cans, cabinets, and doors with safety latches.

Having a clean yard gives your Border Collie a pleasant place to play and discourages bad habits.

after it passes through his system. But the best way to keep your dog from eating his droppings is to make them unavailable—clean up immediately after he eliminates and keep the yard free of stool.

CALLING IN A PROFESSIONAL

Sometimes your Border Collie's bad habits are just too much for you to handle alone. You've tried positive reinforcement, and you've tried corrective approaches, but your Border Collie still won't stop barking or jumping up on your houseguests. It's time to seek professional help if your pup is exhibiting aggressive behavior, such as biting or baring teeth; his destructive chewing is out of control; he cannot be

house-trained; he refuses to obey basic cues; or you feel that you can't control your dog and the safety of others is at risk.

The most effective way to get your misbehaving Border Collie back on track is to enlist the help of a professional dog trainer. Professional dog trainers can be found through referrals from your veterinarian, breeder, or breed club. You can also find trainers through organizations, such as the Association of Pet Dog Trainers (www. apdt.com) or the Certification Council for Professional Dog Trainers (www.ccpdt. org), that allow you to search for trainers iin your area.

To ensure that you and your Border Collie will get the best possible training,

Border Collies have a body language all their own when it comes to working livestock.

select a trainer who has been certified by the CCPDT. To earn the certification, trainers must demonstrate their dog-training knowledge and experience, and they must continue to educate themselves about the latest advances in training techniques and equipment.

BORDER COLLIE BODY LANGUAGE

Dogs don't use words to communicate with humans, but they do use postures and body language to convey their moods. Canine body postures refer to the way that a dog positions his body when he comes into contact with another dog or animal (including humans). The dog's posture signals to the other animal whether the dog is fearful, playful, submissive, or aggressive.

When you can identify the various common postures, you can better understand your Border Collie's behavior and mood, and you can take appropriate action when needed. If your dog is displaying an aggressive posture toward another animal, for example, you can take hold of his leash, walk away calmly, and redirect his attention. Likewise, if another dog strikes an aggressive posture, you and your dog can walk away to prevent a problem. In the following sections, we'll look at common postures and their telltale signs.

Neutral Relaxed

When your Border Collie is in a neutral, relaxed posture, he's simply hanging out, enjoying the day. His head is erect, his ears are up, his tail is relaxed and wagging, his mouth is slightly open, and his weight is evenly distributed over all four feet.

Greeting

Dogs that are saying hello to other dogs approach each other cautiously. The more dominant of the dogs has his ears and tail up, while the more submissive dog has his ears back, his tail down, and his eyes semi-closed.

The two dogs will sniff each other's genital regions as they meet. This may seem rather strange to humans, but to dogs, it's completely natural. Dogs have scent glands on either side of the anus, and these glands contain a scent that's unique to each dog. Dogs sniff at these glands as part of the greeting ritual in an attempt to learn more about each other.

Play Bow

A dog strikes a play bow pose when he wants to let everyone know that he's ready to have some fun. He lowers his front end, including his head and shoulders, and leaves his hips high. His tail is happily wagging, his ears are up, his eyes are soft, his mouth is relaxed, and his tongue is out.

If you want to play with your Border Collie, you can strike the same pose. Lift your hands high and then bring them down in front of you, mimicking his bowing motion. Use an upbeat, positive voice and get ready to toss the ball!

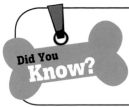

Did You Know?

Indicators of extreme fear in your Border Collie include freezing in place, cowering, having dilated pupils, showing the whites of his eyes, attempting to flee, shedding suddenly, urinating involuntarily, and expressing his anal sac.

Avoid coddling your Border Collie when he's afraid. Your dog's fear combined with an overprotective response from you can reinforce his fear of whatever's frightening him.

Arousal

A dog who has been stimulated by something—whether a sound, a sight, or a smell—will hold the arousal posture with his ears up and forward, his eyes wide open, his tail up, and his weight over his front legs. His muzzle may appear tense, with his lips lifted to expose his teeth, and his hackles (the hairs on the neck and back) may be raised, especially if he's responding to an unfamiliar stimulus.

If he's responding to something pleasurable, however, such as a visit from his best doggy friend, he wags his tail loosely and relaxes his muzzle, and his hackles are down. He knows that something fun is about to happen, and he's ready for it.

Defensive Aggression

If your dog feels threatened, he strikes a defensive aggression posture, warning that he doesn't want to be approached. His hackles may be up, his tail is down and tense, and his ears are back. He carries his weight over his rear legs, his muzzle is tense, and he may snarl and expose his teeth. A dog in this posture may attack or bite if the offender doesn't back down.

Aggressive Attack

A posture that no one likes to see, an aggressive attack pose means that your dog is in fight mode. It's a threatening posture that's intended to frighten, chase away, or prepare to attack intruders. Poorly socialized or highly protective Border Collies may take this pose when they feel that their homes are being invaded or that their humans are threatened.

When your Border Collie is in this posture, you'll see a raised tail and hackles. His ears are erect, tilting forward, and his eyes shoot darts at his adversary. He curls his lips, revealing his teeth. His weight is on his front paws, and he'll likely be charging and barking.

Submission

The opposite of aggression, submission is when a dog defers to a dominant animal. Behaviorists identify two types:

- **Active submission:** The dog tilts his head downward, lowers his tail, cocks his ears back, and closes his eyes halfway. He may raise his paw, and his mouth may be partly closed with the tip of his tongue darting in and out.
- **Passive submission:** The dog lies on his back, exposing his belly. He cocks his ears back, turns his head away, and tucks his tail. This position shows that the dog essentially is surrendering to the other animal.

The *down* position usually indicates that a dog is relaxed.

A dog with separation anxiety exhibits problem behaviors when he's left alone. After his owner leaves, the dog will dig, chew, or scratch at the door trying to get to his owner. He will howl, cry, and bark, and may even urinate or defecate from distress. Though behaviorists don't know exactly why dogs behave this way, they do know that a dog is not punishing his owner for leaving or seeking revenge. Instead, the behaviors are part of a panic response.

Some things seem to trigger separation anxiety. Dogs who are used to being with their owners constantly and are suddenly left alone for the first time may exhibit panicky behavior. A traumatic event, such as time spent in a shelter or kennel, may trigger anxiety. A change in the family's routine or structure, such as a child leaving for college, can also cause stress in the dog's life.

If you believe that your Border Collie is suffering from separation anxiety, here are some ways to remedy the situation:

- Keep your departures and arrivals low-key. Don't give your Border Collie a drawn-out goodbye before you leave or greet him with enthusiastic hugs when you come home. Instead, leave the house quietly and, when you return, ignore the dog for a few minutes before acknowledging him. This will teach him that your comings and goings are just another part of the daily routine.
- Leave your dog with an item of clothing that smells like you. Experts say that an owner's scent will calm a dog's frayed nerves.
- If your dog chews excessively when you're gone, leave him chew toys filled with treats. He will have to work to get the treats out, which should keep him busy—at least for a little while.
- Consider confining him to his crate or a designated dog-proof area of your home when no one is home.

More severe separation anxiety may require you to systematically train your dog to get used to being alone. Discuss options with your veterinarian and trainer; they may be able to offer help with long-term solutions, such as prescription drugs for separation anxiety that can be used during behavior-modification training.

Training your Border Collie in basic obedience is one thing, but teaching him to fly through an agility course, leap for top honors at a disc-dog competition, or drive a flock of sheep takes his training to the next level. Border Collies are born to be active, and you can control your dog's boundless energy and keep his mind sharp by participating in one (or more) of the many events available to canines and their caretakers.

EXERCISE

All dogs need exercise to keep them physically, mentally, and emotionally healthy, and your Border Collie needs plenty of it. As in humans, exercise works a dog's heart and lungs. It strengthens muscles and tendons. It expends pent-up energy, resulting in a more focused (and happily tired) pup. Exercise also challenges the Border Collie to use his brilliant brain; it takes thinking skills to navigate agility equipment, move a flock

Did You Know?

You can become acquainted with the world of competitive dog sport by observing local agility matches, watching obedience competitions, and asking questions of the participants (when they're not competing, of course!) and attendees. Those involved in the hobby will gladly share what they've learned and will likely be delighted to show you the ropes.

of ewes, follow an owner's hand signals, or calculate how far to run and how high to jump to catch a Frisbee. To your Border Collie, exercise is also a fun way for him to spend time with his favorite person—you!

An inactive dog is often overweight and lacks stamina, and he is more likely to strain a joint or tear a ligament when out in the field. An inactive dog is also more prone to destructive behavior and mischief, and thus more likely to get himself into trouble. If your Border Collie has no way to burn off his energy, he'll use his noggin to come up with his own entertainment, which could consist of tearing through your kitchen cabinets or digging up your peonies.

Border Collies must have vigorous exercise every day to be healthy and happy. You can give him the activity he needs by participating in any of the activities described in this chapter, or you could simply take your dog for regular trail hikes, romps on the beach, or jogs around the neighborhood, as long as whatever you do is challenging enough to tire him out and make him use his brain.

BEING A GOOD CITIZEN

Begun in 1989, the American Kennel Club's Canine Good Citizen (CGC) Program is designed to recognize dogs who demonstrate excellent manners at home and in the community. Often held in conjunction with or after puppy kindergarten and basic obedience classes, the program tests dogs on ten obedience exercises, and those who pass earn a certificate from the AKC and can a wear a dog tag bearing the Canine Good Citizen logo.

CGC certification forms the foundation for many competitive sports and other activities, including obedience, agility, tracking, and therapy-dog work. As you train for each exercise of the CGC test, you will solidify your bond with your Border Collie. Plus, the satisfaction of achieving such a goal will likely inspire you to continue training your dog for other events.

Any dog is eligible to participate in CGC, so purebreds and mixed breeds alike can receive certification. Dogs of all ages are welcome to join in the fun, too, although dogs who pass the test as puppies are encouraged to take it again as adults.

To qualify to take the test, you must first sign the AKC's Responsible Dog Owner's Pledge, which affirms that you agree to care for your dog and provide for him in all aspects of his life. It also affirms that you agree to be a responsible dog owner in the community by always cleaning up after your dog and never allowing him to infringe on the rights of others.

After you sign the pledge, you're ready to take the test. You'll need to outfit your dog with a well-fitting buckle or slip collar made of leather, fabric, or chain. The test facilitator will provide a 20-foot leash for the test.

To earn his CGC certificate, your Border Collie has to successfully complete the following ten test items:

1. **Accepting a friendly stranger:** Your dog allows a friendly stranger to approach you and talk to you.
2. **Sitting politely for petting:** Your dog sits next to you and allows a friendly stranger to pet him while he's out with you.
3. **Appearance and grooming:** Your dog allows a stranger to examine and handle him. This test also demonstrates your dedication to your dog's care, as the evaluator examines your Border Collie's overall condition.
4. **Out for a walk:** This exercise shows that you are in control as your Border Collie

Most Border Collies are up for anything when it comes to being active with their owners.

walks attentively beside you on a loose leash while you make right, left, and about turns.

5. **Walking through a crowd:** Your Border Collie demonstrates his ability to walk politely through a crowd of pedestrians on leash.

6. **Sit and down on command and staying in place:** This shows that your Border Collie responds properly to the *sit* and *down* cues and has the ability to stay on cue in either the *sit* or *down* position at the end of a 20-foot line.

7. **Coming when called:** This shows that your dog obeys the *come* command from 10 feet away from you.

8. **Reaction to another dog:** Your Border Collie demonstrates that he behaves appropriately around other dogs.

9. **Reaction to distraction:** The dog shows that he reacts confidently to distracting situations, such as a passing jogger or an object dropped nearby.

10. **Supervised separation:** Your dog shows that he has good manners when left alone with another person for three minutes.

You can find CGC training and testing programs through a local dog club or trainer, or on the AKC's website, www.akc.org.

THE SPORT OF DOGS

Border Collies love to compete in events that test their instincts and learned skills. The AKC, the United Kennel Club (UKC), the various Border Collie clubs, and dozens of specialty clubs across the country hold all sorts of competitive activities, some for dogs of all breeds and some for Border Collies or herding dogs specifically. The Border Collie's natural smarts, speed, athleticism, and herding ability give him the potential for success in many areas of the dog sport. Many types of competition center on not only a dog's abilities but also on how well he can take direction from his handler.

Testing Obedience

If your Border Collie excelled in puppy kindergarten class, conquered basic obedience, and sailed through the Canine Good Citizen test, consider pursuing advanced obedience training toward the goal of participating in competitive obedience trials. This sport requires canine participants to perform specific exercises that show how well they obey their handlers' commands.

The AKC approved its first set of obedience regulations in early 1936 based on guidelines submitted by Helen Whitehouse Walker, a Standard Poodle breeder who pioneered obedience trials in the United States. The AKC and the UKC both offer obedience trials, and dogs who are at least six months old can participate. To be eligible to compete, a dog must be registered or have a limited registration (which allows him to compete in certain non-conformation events) with the organization hosting the trial. The following explanation of competitive obedience is based on the AKC's rules and regulations.

Obedience trials are broken into two categories: all-breed obedience trials, which are open to all breeds and varieties recognized by the AKC; and specialty trials, which are limited to specific breeds or to different varieties of one breed. Both categories have three levels of competition, which progress in difficulty: Novice, Open, and Utility. Each level requires the dogs to complete a specific series of exercises, with each exercise scored individually by a judge.

Exercises at the Novice level, the most basic level of obedience competition, include heel on leash and figure eight, heel free, stand for examination, recall, long sit (one minute), and long down (three minutes). The Open level comprises more complicated exercises to show that the dog can obey both verbal cues and hand signals, including heel free and figure eight, drop on recall, retrieve on the flat, retrieve over a high jump, broad jump, long sit (three minutes), and long down (five minutes). The highest level of competition, Utility includes exercises that demonstrate obedience at its best, including signal exercise, scent discrimination, directed retrieves, moving stand and examination, and directed jumping.

At each level, the dog earns points when he successfully completes an exercise. He must earn at least half of the points possible for each exercise and must earn an

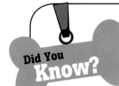

Did You Know?

If you want to compete in AKC trials, but your dog isn't registered with the AKC, you can apply for the Purebred Alternative Listing/Indefinite Listing Privilege (PAL/ILP) program. It allows purebred dogs who are ineligible for AKC registration to participate in many AKC events, including agility, obedience, tracking, rally, and more. After the dog is enrolled in the PAL/ILP program, he is issued a number, which can be used in place of an AKC number on entry forms.

overall score of at least 170 out of a possible 200 points. Each time your dog achieves this goal, he earns one leg toward the title awarded at that particular level. After completing three legs in one level, your dog earns an obedience title for that level.

The available titles tinclude Companion Dog (CD), with three legs in the Novice class; Companion Dog Excellent (CDX), with three legs in the Open class; Utility Dog (UD), with three legs in the Utility class; and Utility Dog Excellent (UDX), with a UD title and ten legs in Open B (open to dogs with CD or CDX titles) and Utility B (open to dogs with CDX or UD titles).

The Obedience Trial Champion (OTCH) title is earned with a UD title, 100 championship points (earned by placing in Open B and Utility B), and a first place in Utility B and Open B, plus a third first-place win in either class. The AKC awards the National Obedience Champion (NOC) title annually to the dog that wins the AKC National Obedience Invitational.

Follow that Scent

Tracking tests a dog's ability to recognize and trace a human's scent, much like dogs do during search and rescue operations. Just because your Border Collie is a herding breed doesn't mean that he can't follow a scent!

AKC tracking began in 1936 as part of the Utility class in obedience competition. It became a separate event in 1947, and the tests have since been refined to include more specific tracking exercises and adjusted to account for the ever-diminishing availability of fields and open spaces.

Tracking tests are typically held in open fields, with the exception of the Variable Surface Tracking exercise, which requires dogs to follow a scent through urban and wilderness environments. The ultimate goal

When selecting dog toys for your Border Collie, make certain they're sized appropriately for your pet. In general, stick with medium to large varieties depending on the toy itself; steer clear of playthings designed for small or giant breeds, as they can be accidentally ingested or too unwieldy.

of tracking is for the dog to locate objects that the tracklayer left behind.

AKC tracking titles are available in the following tests: Tracking Dog (TD), in which the dogs follow a 440- to 500-yard track with three to five changes in direction; Tracking Dog Excellent (TDX), in which the dogs follow a longer (800 to 1,000 yards) and older track with five to seven directional changes and human cross tracks; Variable Surface Tracking (VST), in which the dogs follow a three- to five-hour-old track through an urban or wilderness setting. The Champion Tracker (CT) title is awarded to a dog who has earned the TD, TDX, and VST titles.

A fourth tracking test has been added to the mix for dog owners in urban areas: Tracking Dog Urban (TDU). The intent of this test is to provide dog clubs with an alternative to traditional field tracking tests in areas where such fields are not readily available, to introduce urban dwellers to tracking, and to test dogs' tracking skills in urban environments. Though this is not yet an AKC titling event, the registry encourages clubs to offer it to their members.

Agility Trials

What better way for a Border Collie to expend some energy than to train for agility and participate in agility trials? This fast-growing canine sport challenges your dog's mind and body as he maneuvers through a series of obstacles on a timed course. Your dog responds to your cues as he soars over jumps, races through tunnels, navigates the weave poles, and negotiates other obstacles.

Agility began in England in 1978, and the AKC held its first agility trial in 1994. The UKC offers its own agility trials and titles, and there are a number of national agility clubs, such as the United States Dog Agility Association and the North American Dog Agility Council, that offer agility education and titling events.

Agility classes, titles, and obstacles vary from organization to organization, but common obstacles include the A-frame, the teeter, bar jumps, tire jumps, tunnels, and weave poles. The handler runs the course with his or her dog, giving cues and signals to guide the dog through the course with accuracy and speed.

Training for agility can be a challenge for many owners because the obstacles take up a considerable amount of room, but there are agility clubs across the country that have practice facilities where you can learn with, train with, and enjoy the mutual support and encouragement of club members. Some clubs also hold practice matches. If agility competition interests you, look for training classes or agility clubs in your area where you can get started.

Rally Together

If you and your Border Collie think you want to try your hand—or paw—at agility or obedience trials, but you're not sure if you're ready yet, AKC rally could be the sport for you. Rally combines competitive obedience with elements of agility in a less formal testing scenario than that of an obedience trial.

Rally allows you and your Border Collie to move at your own pace through the course, which typically includes ten to twenty stations; each station is marked by a sign that indicates the exercise to perform at that station. Scoring is not as rigorous as in traditional obedience, and communication and teamwork between you and your dog is highly encouraged.

As with the other canine sports, dogs can earn titles and progress through different levels as they develop their skills. Titles include Rally Novice, Rally Advanced, Rally Excellent, and Rally Advanced Excellent.

Conformation Showing

If you're like most Border Collie owners, you probably think that your dog looks perfect—or very close to perfect! His markings make him unique, his temperament is top-notch, and his physique is in a class by itself.

Conformation trials—what most people know as "dog shows"—give you the opportunity to see and interact firsthand with other beautiful purebred dogs. Unless your Border Collie is of showing or breeding quality, your breeder will have required you to have your pet neutered or spayed, in which case your dog is not eligible to compete against the other four-legged beauties. You can still attend dog shows, though, to appreciate the sport and see your favorite breed in action.

One of the most well-known conformation shows, the Westminster Kennel Club Dog Show, held annually in February at Madison Square Garden in New York City, has been showcasing the best of the best since 1877. The show was initiated by a group of hunting-dog fanciers who frequently met at the Westminster Hotel in Manhattan and formed

SMART TIP!

Make your Border Collie's day by taking him on a hike. The sights and sounds of the outdoors will engage his senses and tire him out. Have him carry his own water and supplies by outfitting him with a lightweight canine backpack.

the Westminster Kennel Club, one of the first kennel clubs in the United States with the purpose of showing dogs.

Border Collies who compete in dog shows are judged on how well they meet the breed standard, which describes the ideal physical representation of the breed as set forth by the hosting organization. The standard of the Border Collie Society of America, the AKC parent club for the breed, is used at all AKC-sanctioned shows.

Conformation dog shows are organized in various ways. All-breed shows offer competition for all of the breeds recognized by the registry hosting the show, such as the AKC or the UKC. Specialty shows are often hosted by breed clubs to offer competition for one specific breed or for varieties of a single breed. Group shows are limited to dogs within a particular variety group. The Border Collie belongs to the AKC's Herding Group and competes against other herding breeds, such as the Australian Shepherd, the German Shepherd Dog, and the Pembroke and Cardigan Welsh Corgis, at group shows.

The judges who evaluate the dogs must be experts in the breeds they are judging. In the ring, the judge will examine the dogs from head to toe; feel their bones, muscles, and coat texture; examine their teeth, eyes, and ears; view the dogs in profile to look

for overall balance; and watch the dogs in motion to assess their gait.

The judge awards placements to the dogs who adhere most closely to their respective breed standards. Winning dogs earn points toward their championship titles and colorful ribbons to decorate their walls.

MORE ORGANIZED FUN

Outside of the kennel-club circuit, you can engage your dog in other organized sporting events. Some of the activities that your Border Collie loves and is naturally good at, such as running, fetching, and disc-catching, can be parlayed into competitive fun, awards, and titles.

Flyball

Flyball is a timed relay race that pits two teams of four dogs against each other. At the signal, the first dog on each team runs down a lane, jumping over a series of hurdles on the way to a box with a lever. The dog steps on the lever, which sends a tennis ball flying. The dog then catches the ball and runs back down the lane, jumping the hurdles again, to return the ball to his handler. At that point, the next dog takes off to repeat the process—and so on until all four canine team members have had their turn. The team that completes the relay first is the winner. This fun activity can burn a lot of Border Collie energy!

A group of trainers in Southern California invented flyball in the late 1960s and 1970s. By the 1980s, the sport was enjoying huge popularity, thanks in part to a spot on the *Tonight Show with Johnny Carson*. The first flyball organization, the North American Flyball Association (NAFA), was formed in 1984 to design uniform competition rules and tout the sport as one

A spectacular catch! The Border Collie's high-flying antics make him a disc-dog star.

that could be enjoyed by virtually every dog. A newer organization, the United Flyball League International (UFLI), was formed in 2004. The sport currently enjoys international representation, with clubs in the United States, South Africa, Australia, and the United Kingdom.

If your Border Collie loves to catch tennis balls, seek out a flyball club in your area. You can find a list of local clubs on the NAFA website, www.flyball.org, or on the United Flyball League International website, www.u-fli.com.

Disc Dog

The sport of disc dog took off in popularity when Wham-O introduced the Frisbee in the late 1950s to delighted outdoor enthusiasts. It skyrocketed in 1974 when a nineteen-year-old college student and his dog jumped the fence at a nationally televised baseball game between the Los Angeles Dodgers and the Cincinnati Reds. The man, Alex Stein of Ohio, tossed a few discs for his dog, Ashley Whippet, who amazed the fans with his speed and jumping ability. The crowd—as well as the new sport—went wild. Today, the Ashley Whippet Invitational is a prestigious international tournament named after the famous disc-catching dog in 1982, culminating each year in the Frisbee Dog World Championship.

Though you can toss a flying disc for your pup to fetch wherever you please, you can participate in competitions that test your Border Collie's disc-catching ability. Teams typically consist of a dog and owner, and standard competitive events are the "toss and fetch" and "freestyle."

In the toss and fetch, teams have one minute to make as many throws as possible on a field. They are awarded points for catches based on the distances of the throws, and extra points are given for midair catches. Freestyle events feature choreographed routines that showcase the team's style. Routines are judged subjectively in categories including canine athleticism, degree of difficulty, and showmanship. Freestyle routines often include flips and other acrobatics along with disc-catching, of course, and fast-moving fun.

Disc dog clubs exist throughout the country. Winners of local and regional competitions can strive to compete in one of the national or worldwide competitions, such as the Frisbee Dog World Championship. Since the sport officially began in 1975, a Border Collie has been named champion eight times—the most for any one breed.

TRAINING TO HERD

If a Border Collie could choose his ideal vocation, it would be—what else?—herding. There's nothing like watching a skilled Border Collie at work in the field. With his innate instincts, the dog will circle livestock and control the animals with his intense, almost hypnotic, gaze. He'll outguess his charges' every move and head off any

that try to break away. He'll move silently through the grass to not spook the livestock. It's as if he were born to herd—and he was!

Training your Border Collie to herd takes know-how coupled with years of refinement. Though your Border Collie is an instinctive herder, the skill and technique involved in training and handling a dog in the field takes time and patience—and much more detail than can be presented here. Consult with your breeder or a breed club for more information about the art of handling your herder.

Though it is a very specialized skill, you can try your hand at herding at home. Here's some basic information to help you find out if your dog has what it takes to drive sheep. Even if you don't plan to work your Border Collie, you may still want to train your dog so that you can participate in the competitive herding events offered by the various kennel clubs and breed clubs.

The Round Pen

Once your Border Collie has mastered basic obedience and knows how to walk on a leash, come when called, and perform the *down*, *sit*, and *stay* exercises, you can introduce him to livestock. Most trainers recommend using ducks or gentle lambs until the dog understands directional cues.

To begin, you'll need a cane or bamboo pole, which is used to keep the dog wide and issue directions, and a round pen made from chicken wire or hardware cloth to contain the ducks or lambs.

Put your dog on leash and walk up to the pen. Some dogs may be a bit rough when first introduced to livestock, so give your Border Collie the *down/stay* command. When he obeys and seems comfortable around the critters, he's ready to learn basic flanking cues.

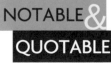
NOTABLE & QUOTABLE

Power is the dog's ability to move livestock, either by threat or by backing up the threat through biting. A truly powerful dog seldom needs to bite; the livestock can see in the dog's movements and actions that he's not afraid. They can read the power and see the determination in the dog. They know they must move.

—Bruce Fogt, Border Collie owner, trainer, and author of Lessons from a Stock Dog

Flanking cues direct your dog to circle to his left or right. The Border Collie's instinct is to stay on the opposite side of the flock or herd from you, his pack leader. Because the animals are in a circular pen, he should keep running to the opposite side of the pen from you. Any well-bred Border Collie will do this instinctually. Here's how to teach your dog to go left or right:

- **Go-bye:** The *go-bye* cue tells your dog to circle to his left. First, put your dog in a down and leave him. Return and approach him, walking in the direction that you want him to go, which is to his left, and give the *go-bye* cue.
- **Way-to-me:** The *way-to-me* cue tells your dog to circle to his right. Follow the same steps as in the *go-bye* cue, but when you approach your Border Collie and give the *way-to-me* cue, walk toward his right instead.

As the pup grasps the flanking cues, gradually decrease the number of steps you take toward him until you can remain in one place while giving the verbal cues.

In addition to flanking, you can also teach your dog to outrun, which means that he takes a wide, pear-shaped or semi-circular course to get him to the far side of the flock without alarming the livestock. Driving, which means that the dog gets behind the sheep to drive them away from the handler, is not natural to the Border Collie and must be trained, as the breed's instinct is to push the livestock toward the handler.

Out in the Field

Dogs that have mastered herding ducks or lambs in a pen are ready to work in a small field or paddock area. Experts recommend using calm, gentle animals, such as lambs that are used to being handled by dogs; older rams, ewes, and cattle can be aggressive and shouldn't be used for training. At this point, it is wise to seek the help of a trainer if you're not experienced in working with herding dogs.

A trainer will build on the lessons learned in the pen, teaching your dog to drive the livestock toward you, steer the sheep right or left, and outrun and fetch wayward ewes. More advanced techniques include using whistle cues in place of verbal commands, training the dog to drive, teaching the dog to pen and take sheep through obstacles, and showing the dog how to shed, which means to separate a group of sheep from the flock.

BECOMING A THERAPY DOG

Organized activities don't have to be competitive to be rewarding. For those Border Collies (and their owners) who enjoy giving back to the community, becoming a therapy dog is an opportunity to bring joy to nursing-home residents, hospital patients, sick children, and others who may benefit from the companionship of a dog.

Well-behaved Border Collies who have their Canine Good Citizen certificates are on their way to becoming therapy dogs. Different from service dogs, who assist disabled owners, therapy dogs make informal visits to people in nursing homes and patients of all ages in hospitals. Some therapy dogs participate in more structured sessions with people who are receiving physical rehabilitation.

Organizations such as Therapy Dogs International (www.tdi-dog.org) and Delta Society (www.deltasociety.org) evaluate potential dog-and-handler therapy teams. Therapy dogs must display sound temperament and be patient, confident, and at ease

Herding Terms

Helpful herding terms include:

- **Down:** The cue that tells the dog to drop instantly to the ground.
- **Driving:** When the dog is positioned between the sheep and the handler and herds the sheep away from the handler.
- **Fetching:** When the dog drives the sheep to the handler from behind them.
- **Gathering:** When the dog collects the sheep from their scattered grazing positions and moves them into a compact group.
- **Heeling:** When the dog nips and bites at the feet and legs of livestock.
- **Lift:** The pause between the outrun and the start of the fetch.

- **Singling:** When the dog separates one animal from the flock or herd.
- **Wearing:** When a dog keeps the livestock following his handler. A Border Collie will do this naturally without cues, but handlers often use commands such as *walk on up*, which instructs the dog to walk toward the sheep and force them to move, and *steady*, which tells the dog to slow down to a creeping walk.

A cue that virtually all herding-dog handlers use to tell their dogs that it's time for a break is *that will do*. This command releases the dog from his charges and also communicates to the dog that he should leave the stock alone.

in a variety of environments, from busy hospital wards to quiet retirement homes. They should thrive on human contact, because one of a therapy dog's main purposes is to allow people to pet him, hug him, and shower him with attention. Of course, therapy dogs must also be clean, healthy, and flea-free.

Different organizations have different requirements for screening, testing, and certifying dogs as therapy dogs. If you and your Border Collie are interested in

pursuing this altruistic endeavor, look for a recognized organization, such as one of the aforementioned, with affiliates or volunteers in your area.

Anecdotal and clinical evidence has shown that when someone holds or pets an animal, his or her blood pressure drops and stress level decreases. Pets can also pull people out of depression. Your Border Collie brings you joy at home, so why not share that joy with others in need?

Smart owners can find out more about the breed through the following organizations. Members will be glad to help you dig deeper into the world of Border Collies—you won't even have to beg!

Academy of Veterinary Homeopathy: A membership of veterinarians and veterinary students devoted to education and research in veterinary homeopathy and certifying veterinary homeopaths. www.theavh.org

American Animal Hospital Association: The AAHA accredits small animal hospitals throughout the United States and Canada. www.healthypet.com

American Border Collie Association: This registry promotes the working ability of the breed. www.americanbordercollie.org

American Dog Owners Association: A nationwide group of dog owners and fanciers who promote responsible ownership and owners' rights. www.adoa.org

American Holistic Veterinary Medical Association: This professional organization for holistic veterinarians promotes alternative healthcare techniques and supports research in the field. www.ahvma.org

American Humane Association: This nonprofit organization founded in 1877 is dedicated to protecting children and animals. www.americanhumane.org

American Kennel Club: Founded in 1884, the AKC is America's oldest purebred dog registry. It governs conformation, companion, and performance events and promotes responsible dog ownership. www.akc.org

American Kennel Club Canine Health Foundation: This foundation is the largest nonprofit funder of exclusively canine research in the world. www.akcchf.org

American Society for the Prevention of Cruelty to Animals: The ASPCA was the first humane organization in North America. Its mission, as stated by Henry Bergh in 1866, is "to provide effective means for the prevention of cruelty to animals throughout the United States." www.aspca.org

American Veterinary Medical Association: This nonprofit association represents more than 80,000 veterinarians and is the accrediting body for American veterinary schools. www.avma.org

ASPCA Animal Poison Control Center: This resource offers an informative website with lists of pet toxins and FAQs, as well as a hotline for animal poison-related emergencies that is available 24 hours a day at 888-426-4435. A consultation fee may be charged. www.aspca.org/apcc

Association of American Feed Control Officials: The AAFCO develops and implements uniform and equitable laws, regulations, standards, and enforcement policies for the manufacture, distribution and sale of animal feeds, resulting in safe and useful feeds. www.aafco.org

Association of Pet Dog Trainers: This international organization for professional dog trainers fosters continuing education among its members. www.apdt.com

Border Collie Society of America: The AKC parent club sponsors events and offers breeder referral, a rescue program, advice for potential owners, breed education, and much more. www.border colliesociety.com

Canadian Kennel Club: Our northern neighbor's oldest kennel club is similar to the AKC in the States. www.ckc.ca

Canine Freestyle Federation: A volunteer organization devoted to promoting the sport of canine freestyle (dancing with dogs) and holding demonstrations and competitions. www.canine-freestyle.org

Delta Society: This nonprofit trains and tests therapy-dog teams and aids in the implementation of animal-assisted therapy programs. www.deltasociety.org

Dog Scouts of America: Take your dog to camp. www.dogscouts.com

Fédération Cynologique Internationale: This international canine organization includes eighty-four member countries and partners that all issue their own pedigrees and train their own judges. www.fci.be

International Sheepdog Society: Based in the United Kingdom, this registry advocates maintaining the breed's working ability. www.isds.org.uk

Love on a Leash: Share your dog's love with others. www.loveonaleash.org

National Association of Professional Pet Sitters: When you will be away for a while, hire someone to watch and entertain your dog. www.petsitters.org

North American Dog Agility Council: NADAC was founded in 1993 and holds competitive agility events through its sanctioned clubs. www.nadac.com

North American Flyball Association: NAFA was established in 1984 and is recognized as the world's governing body for the sport of flyball. www.flyball.org

Pet Care Services Association: A nonprofit trade association that includes nearly 3,000 American and international pet-care businesses. www.petcareservices.org

Pet Sitters International: This group's mission is to educate professional pet sitters and promote, support, and recognize excellence in pet sitting and to provide reliable pet sitters. www.petsit.com

Therapy Dogs International: This volunteer organization tests and certifies dog-and-owner therapy teams. www.tdi-dog.org

United Kennel Club: Established in 1898, this international purebred registry emphasizes performance events and education. www.ukcdogs.com

United States Border Collie Club: This organization is dedicated to preserving the breed as a working stock dog and hosts a website with a wealth of information. www.bordercollie.org

United States Dog Agility Association: This international organization founded in 1986 introduced the sport of agility to America; its Grand Prix tournament is one of the most prestigious competitions in the sport. www.usdaa.com

World Canine Freestyle Organization: This nonprofit promotes canine freestyle around the world for competition and entertainment. www.worldcaninefreestyle.org

ON THE ROAD

Traveling with your Border Collie can be fun, as long as you're prepared. Whether you're traveling across town or across the country, knowing what to bring along and how to prepare will make the trip enjoyable.

Before you hit the road, you'll need to accustom your Border Collie to the car. These exercises should ideally begin when your dog is a puppy, though adult dogs can learn this trick, too.

First, gather your supplies. You'll need a crate or another restraining device, such as a car safety harness made for dogs, to keep your Border Collie safe in the event of an accident. He should be wearing his collar, with ID tags attached. You'll also need a blanket or pillow for comfort, your dog's leash, some plastic bags and paper towels for accident clean-up, and some food and water for longer trips.

When you initially introduce the dog to your vehicle, let him investigate the car inside and out. Next, tell him to hop into his crate, which has his favorite chew toy or a

tasty treat inside to entice him, or strap him in to the safety harness. If using your Border Collie's crate, close the crate door. Then, hop into the front seat and just sit there, praising your Border Collie for being a good dog. Do this exercise a few times and, if your dog is OK with it, progress to turning on the engine while you're parked. Next, drive him around the block, praising him and encouraging him with an upbeat tone. In most cases, Border Collies love on-the-road adventures. If your dog seems anxious, shakes, or gets sick, however, you'll need to slow down the training process until he feels comfortable with each step.

No matter how short the trip, make sure your Border Collie is secure in the car, either in his crate or harness. Resist the temptation to let your dog run free in the car. This is a distraction, putting you, your passengers, and other drivers on the road in danger,

Whenever your dog is in someone else's care, be sure to provide the person or facility with your contact information; your veterinarian's name, phone number, and after-hours or emergency number; the names and doses of any medications that your Border Collie is taking; the name and contact information of a nearby friend or relative; and any other important information. Be sure to alert the caretaker if your dog has any allergies or medical issues.

and it is hazardous to your dog. If you stop quickly or get into an accident with your dog loose in the car, he could be launched against the side of the car or out an open window. Some areas have laws that require dogs to be restrained in moving vehicles; check for specific regulations in your area.

Longer trips require a little more planning and packing. Your Border Collie will need enough food to last for the journey, along with treats and bottled water. Pack the supplies you'll need to keep up with routine grooming, including his toothbrush and toothpaste, any medications your dog is taking, and a portable first-aid kit. Be sure that you have your dog's ID tags, and bring along an extra collar and leash. To keep your dog occupied and comfortable, bring some of his favorite toys and some soft bedding. It's also a good idea to bring his veterinary records, including proof of vaccinations.

As you travel, stop every few hours to let your Border Collie relieve himself. Though some rest stops have designated pet areas, these patches may not be very clean if they're frequented by many dogs, some of which may be unvaccinated. Instead, choose clean areas and pick up your dog's messes. Offer your Border Collie water whenever you stop, and feed him if it's mealtime.

Talk to your veterinarian about any additional vaccinations that your Border Collie might need before your trip, depending on your destination.

HOME ALONE

No matter how hard it is, there will be times when you won't be able to travel with your Border Collie. Business trips, visiting sick relatives, long work days, or other circumstances might require you to leave your dog behind for a few days, or at least home alone for longer than usual on a given day. In these situations, you'll need to make sure that your Border Collie is well taken care of.

Your dog can stay at a boarding kennel, which is a facility where dogs stay overnight for an extended period of time. Each dog stays in his own separate area, which may or may not have access to an individual fenced run. The kennel staff cares for the dogs, feeding them at scheduled intervals, making sure that they have clean water, walking them regularly, and cleaning up the kennel areas. Some boarding kennels offer extras, such as hikes, playtime, and grooming. Here are points to consider when choosing a boarding kennel:

- Is the facility recommended by your vet?
- Are the runs large? Are they clean? Do the dogs have full bowls of fresh water? Are the smaller dogs separated from the larger dogs if group playtime is offered? Inspect the facility before you commit to leaving your dog there.
- What are the regular hours of operation, and pick-up/drop-off times?

- What types of vaccinations are required, and what health documentation must owners provide for their dogs?
- Does the kennel offer special services, such as individual walks or grooming, if requested?
- How much experience does the staff have with Border Collies?
- Can you bring items from home, such as your dog's bed? Do they allow you to provide your own food?
- Do they check incoming dogs for fleas and ticks, and do they offer a flea bath before your dog goes home?
- Is a veterinarian on the premises or on-call in case of emergency?

Another option is a dog sitter, an individual who cares for your dog while you're away for a short or extended period of time. A dog sitter's role will vary depending on your needs. He or she may come to your house and check in on your Border Collie several times during the day, taking him to the bathroom, giving him some exercise and companionship, filling his food and water bowls, and making sure that all is well. He or she may stay at your home while you're away, providing house-sitting services at the same time, or the person may care for your dog at his or her own home. A dog sitter can often be a better option than a kennel because your dog will be able to remain at home in familiar surroundings or stay in a comfortable home setting.

When hiring a dog sitter, interview several, and have each one meet your Border Collie. You'll know right away if your dog likes the person. During the interview, ask for references, whether he or she belongs to any professional organizations (such as the National Association of Professional Pet Sitters), how much experience the pet sitter has had with Border Collies, and how long he or she has been a pet sitter. Find out if the sitter is insured and bonded, and ask about his or her experience with medical care and canine first aid.

Discuss the exact services that the pet sitter will provide, the hours that he or she will be staying at your home or dropping by to care for your dog, and the charges for his or her services.

DOGGY DAY CARE

A doggy day care facility is a place where dogs go for care and activity during the day, usually while their owners are at work, rather than for overnight stays. Trained staff members watch over the canine clients, who run around and play together in an open setting, socializing and interacting with other dogs. Many doggy day cares have play areas, shallow swimming pools, lounging areas, spa (well, grooming) services, and more—in fact, some can be quite posh!

When looking for a doggy day care, try to find a facility that is conveniently located to your home or office and that has hours of operation that work with your daily schedule. Do your homework and interview the owner or manager, ask for and call references, and find out how much experience the staff has with Border Collies. Also ask the manager to take you on a tour of the premises. Is everything clean and well maintained? Are staff members interacting with the dogs? Do the dogs seem happy?

Ask which vaccinations (and possibly flea and tick preventives) the facility requires, as well as about any additional services that the business may offer, such as grooming, training, or routine veterinary care. Find out if the facility offers drop-in service or if you need to put your dog on a regular weekly schedule of set days and times.

BORDER COLLIE, a Smart Owner's Guide®

LIBRARY OF CONGRESS CATALOGING-IN-PUBLICATION DATA

Bedwell-Wilson, Wendy.
  Border collie / by Wendy Bedwell Wilson
    p. cm. -- (Smart owner's guide)
  Includes bibliographical references and index.
  ISBN 978-1-59378-782-0
  1. Border collie. I. Kennel Club Books. II. Title.
  SF429.B64B67 2012
  636.737′4--dc23

                    2011031135

JOIN
Club
Border
TODAY!